MOOSE TRACKS

The secret history of the Jones family in Victor, Idaho

RUSSELL JONES

Copyright © 2014 by Russell Jones

All rights reserved. Printed in the United States

No part of this book may be used or reproduced in any manner whatsoever without written permission from the author except in the case of brief quotations embodied in critical articles or reviews.

ISBN 978-0-9773354-1-1

www.code22west.com

Cover design and page layout by Pete Valle

Printed in the United States by Morris Publishing®
3212 East Highway 30
Kearney, NE 68847
1-800-650-7888

TABLE OF CONTENTS

PROLOGUE	1
SKELETONS IN OUR CLOSET	5
A DOLLAR AND A LOT OF LOVE	15
OH MY HELL!!	21
SONS OF BITTIES AND SURLY BADGERS	29
AN ADDED MEASURE OF SURLINESS	43
HISTORY REPEATING ITSELF	49
SEEING THINGS AND HEARING THINGS	55
MORE LIKE FIONA THAN SNOW WHITE	65
MOOSE-EATING COUSINS	69
HE WAS WILLIE, I WAS SANDY	91
SHE WAS A KILLER	103
DEAD AND BLOODY CARCASSES	115
SPECTACLE OF NATURE	119
THE GHOST MOOSE	125
THE MOST EERILY SAD THING	135
THE OXYMORONS ARRIVE	141
MOM KNEW HOW TO COOK	143
TESTING MY DAD	155
THE GREAT VICTOR DOG MASSACRE	161
MY RELIGIOUS ENIGMA	167
KENNY FELL IN LOVE	179
THE HARROP'S HILL HITCHHIKER	191
PAYING FOR MY MOOSE	195

*To my children,
and their children,
and their children,
forever and ever...*

And, to my nephew James

PROLOGUE

I love my family, both roots and branches, and I am proud of my place in it. I like to describe my youth as Tom Sawyerish, except that Tom Sawyer was a little tame. While my brothers and sisters and I didn't exactly run wild, we had a lot of freedom, far more than my children and grand children. The circumstances of modern living robbed my children of many of the things I took for granted as a child. As a boy I ranged far and wide with instructions to check in now and then and be home for dinner. My grandchildren are even more shackled than my children because our society has become so dangerous to children.

I asked Mom once, when I was eight or nine, if our family was poor. I observed at that time that she and Dad struggled to pay the bills.

"We don't have much money," Mom admitted. Then, she led me outside and pointed to the mountains that surrounded our little town. "Few boys in the world have a backyard like that," she said.

She pointed to the horses in our pasture. "Not everyone has horses to ride."

She then pointed to the fishing poles leaning against the house. "How many boys your age go fishing whenever they want? Or hike to Mud Lake to catch frogs? You have a warm bed to sleep in and plenty to eat. Do you feel poor?"

As a youth, I didn't know much of my family's history. Since then I've at least learned some of our ancestors' names and a few stories. They intrigue me, those who have gone before ... the Joneses, the Lotts, the Moores and the Jemmetts, the Farnsworths, Harmons, Haskins, Elmers, Goddards, Wrights, and on and on. Since coming to this hemisphere, there were many laborers, some sailors and soldiers, but mainly they were farmers and homemakers. No presidents, senators or governors. No statesmen or writers, scientists, at least not in the past three or four hundred years. There are, however, many pioneers and settlers—men and women constantly spreading out, looking for elbow room, searching for something better over the next hill, mountain, plain or ocean.

I like my ancestors. Sometimes they feel close, as though they are looking over my shoulder to make sure I don't screw it all up. The sum of their traits, genes and characteristics were evident in my parents and, presumably, are likewise visible in me. Some are happy-go-lucky and jovial, others serious and grumpy; and still others are a little of both. They were strong and tenacious in some ways and weak and vulnerable in others. They are, after all, the reason I and my siblings are who we are. Their choices constructed our family culture and determined where we would be born and live. They helped shape my character in a way I hope is good for those who follow me. In the final analysis, I hope the choices I have made, and will make, represent them well.

I say that because of the way I have chosen to tell this story. I have written this intending to preserve and pass on to my children and grandchildren some stories of my youth and memories of my parents, brothers and sisters, as well as my hopes, struggles and dreams. Sometimes I use unconventional terms when referring to myself and my family. I have struggled with some of the words I have used. I wrote them, deleted them, rewrote them and finally let them stay. I am at peace with those words. Some who read this will not be. I want you to understand I do it with the utmost affection and without any animosity at all. It's an attempt to explain why I and my siblings are the way we are. I have no intention of belittling anyone or dredging up old sores and grudges. I embellish all my stories and I offer no apologies for that. If you don't like the way I tell it, please feel free to write your own version.

After my great, great grandparents made their ways across the plains with the other Mormon pioneers, they took up residence in the Rocky Mountains because at that time it was one of the few pieces of real estate on earth that no one else wanted. In those days, society in the eastern United States didn't take kindly to our sort. Some of them wanted to exterminate us. After looking around for a few years, my ancestors decided that the higher in the mountains they could get, the better. So they finally decided to live in a little valley on the western edge of the Tetons in one of the most beautiful, but cold and inhospitable climates in the world.

    Let it never be said that my family values creature comforts over aesthetics. As evidence I point out that for the past one hundred and fifteen years, we chose to live in the top of the mountains where the oxygen is thin and the animals are thinner, but where the scenery is beautiful. We adapted and our family grew.

    We solved some of life's problems and inconveniences along the way, but certainly not all of them. There are many mysteries to life, things far beyond my ability to explain. My ancestors passed down to me a strong sense of family. They also passed on certain ways of doing things, particular beliefs, behaviors and hopes. Along with those things they passed on a lot of questions. Those questions remain with me and you'll see them pop up if you read on. I don't have answers to all of those questions, but I believe there are answers. If I continue to believe the things that have been given to me, I'll get all the answers eventually. If I don't believe, then I won't get the answers, because those who won't believe will never see.

SKELETONS IN OUR CLOSET

Dad took Kenny and me up Mike Harris Canyon one summer day when we were small. I was six and Kenny four. We hiked on a dirt road that meandered up the bottom of the canyon. We didn't get far because of all the distractions—bugs, sticks, moss on trees and an occasional noisy squirrel. Dad helped us find some pretty rocks to put in our pockets for Mom to add to the treasures we collected for her, and then he sniffed out a huckleberry bush where we sat and munched on berries for a while. Dad was good at that. Years later, I learned he could smell huckleberries two canyons over through chainsaw exhaust and with the wind blowing.

Kenny and I were concerned about bears and mountains lions but that added to the allure of the forest. We scampered about chasing butterflies and hiding from each other, unafraid of anything because Dad was right there. We sensed there was not a creature in the forest that would challenge our father. And if one did, woe be unto it. On our way back to the truck we tiptoed on rocks across a small stream that intersected the road. On the other side, Dad knelt and pointed to some tracks in the soft, moist dirt. Little heart-shaped indentations framed the edge of the stream.

"Deer tracks," Dad said.

Kenny pointed to a track that was quite a lot larger. "Is that a deer track?" he asked skeptically.

"Moose," Dad replied. "Probably a cow or a small bull. A big bull's track would be larger."

We diverted from the road and followed a game trail that took us over a small ridge. From there we could see the bottom of the canyon where the stream flowed. It was covered with willows and tall grass. Pine trees poked up here and there.

"Looky there," Dad said.

About one hundred yards away a moose ambled through the willows, stopping occasionally to reach down and get a soggy mouthful before rising up to chew and look around lazily before lowering its head for another bite. We moved closer and sat down to watch. The moose was as big as Lady, our horse, but black and with antlers. Its rack was about the same size as Dad's open hands.

"Young bull," Dad said.

Ken and I had seen deer and elk before but this was our first moose. We started asking questions.

"Are moose mean? Why is it black? Is it dumb?"

The moose heard us, raised his head and stared for a long moment, as if perturbed we would suggest it was dumb, before deciding we were not a threat and resuming his meal.

"Some people say moose are awkward and dumb,"

Dad said. "Sometimes they seem tame. They can be as timid as deer and as skittish as a bull elk. If he got angry with you he could put his hoof right through your rib cage. This moose right here could jump any fence in Victor and, if he wanted, could disappear into the forest in a few seconds."

We watched quietly a few more minutes before hiking back to the truck and driving home. The moose never left while we were there.

When we got home, Mom had supper ready. We almost always had potatoes. Mom prepared them in a variety of ways, but nine times out of ten we had bread, potatoes, a vegetable, usually green beans because they were easy to grow and can. And meat. We always had meat. On that particular night we sat down at our kitchen table and had fried potatoes, green beans and in the middle of the table was a plateful of steaks, some large and some small that Mom had coated in flour and fried in lard with salt and pepper.

As we ate Dad told Mom about the moose we saw up the canyon.

That got Kenny and me asking more questions about moose. And since we were eating an obvious question arose.

"Are moose good to eat?" Kenny asked.

"What do you think?" Dad said, chewing on a mouthful of steak.

I remembered the big, black moose with its antlers and the long moose stare it had given us.

"I don't think moose would taste good," I said, swallowing.

Kenny gave me that I-can't-believe-you're-almost-two-years-older-than-me look and Mom and Dad grinned at each other.

That night after dinner our family sat together on the couch in the living room. At that point there were six of us including four children–me, Kenny, Cathy who was about two, and Tommy, who was one.

Mom had just put Tom and Cathy to bed and was trying to get Kenny and me there too. I was sitting on Dad's lap and Ken was on Mom's. We still were excited about the moose and Kenny was explaining to Mom what a moose track looked like by drawing a moose track shape in the air with his finger. He was not satisfied with the results and repeatedly drew it and then tried again. Finally, Dad put his index fingers and thumbs together to form the shape Kenny was looking for.

"Is this it? Dad said.

"Yes." Kenny said. "Mom, moose tracks look like that, pointing to the shape Dad was making with his hands."

"That looks like a heart to me," Mom said.

"That's what moose tracks look like," Kenny repeated. "Hearts. Moose tracks look like hearts. When I grow up I want to make big tracks like a moose."

"You've already left moose tracks in my heart," Mom said. "I'm sure you'll make plenty more."

We lived in Victor, Idaho. Population: 241. My Dad was born in Victor and Mom said he would never leave. And why should he? Victor was the perfect place for him. I think God made it with us Joneses in mind. Victor is surrounded by mountains. To the east the Idaho-Wyoming state line runs the length of Teton Valley and the Tetons rise up to more than 13,000 feet above sea level with a range that extends north to Yellowstone National Park. On the south is the Palisades range stretching out 20 to 30 miles to the South Fork of the Snake River. West of Victor is still another mountain range we called the Big Holes that form a natural division between Teton Valley and the Upper Snake River Valley of eastern Idaho. North of Victor is open valley, farmland, ranch land and two more small towns, Driggs and Tetonia, both very much like Victor.

Victor has an elementary school where I and my siblings attended elementary school. Immediately east of the school is the next largest building in town, the LDS or Mormon meetinghouse where the Victor First Ward held services every Sunday. Victor also had a train depot, a few small stores and a combined café and bar called the Timberline, the fourth largest building in town, also wryly referred to by the area's inactive Mormons as the Victor Second Ward.

When I tell people I was weaned on moose meat, they usually wink at me and chuckle in a way that says they think I'm kidding.

Some of them will say: "Yeah, me too" as though it's a joke. After all, unless you're lucky enough to draw one of the few tags the Idaho Department of Fish and Game offers each year, it's unlikely you ever will get a taste of moose meat, let alone be weaned on it unless someone in your family has a knack for finding moose in just the right place at just the right time. We had someone in our family who did that. Moose was one of our family staples.

In Victor, winters are long and summers short. The growing season extends from Memorial Day to Labor Day in a good year. Victor is not the most fertile part of the Lord's vineyard. The ground is hard and rocky, probably the result of a glacier depositing its moraine back in the ice age. Speaking of the ice age, it never really ended in Victor. Snow usually falls in November, but can arrive in October to stay throughout winter. It normally melts from the valley floor sometime in March or April. While the summers are cool and pleasant, snow can fall in any month including July and August. At 6,100 feet in elevation, frost also is common in summer so gardening is chancy, as is farming. Green beans grow well there, as do peas and potatoes. Tomatoes and cucumbers have little chance unless you have a greenhouse, which we didn't. My hat is off to farmers in Victor. They earn every dollar they make. Every year they plant is a gamble.

Chokecherries grow wild along the creeks and huckleberries can be harvested in the mountains in late July and early August. When they first arrived in the valley in the 1890s, the Joneses grew most of what they ate and partook of the abundant wildlife including deer, elk, and of course, moose.

As a youth my Dad became an expert fly fisherman. When I was young, he would go fishing every day after he got off work and when I got old enough I always wanted to go with him. I would dig worms and have my fishing pole ready when he arrived at home in the late afternoon. Most often, we'd go to the river on the west side in the little farming community of Cedron, also known as Kunzville.

The thing I remember clearest about my Dad is how hard he worked. He attacked work like it was an enemy. In the words of one of his colorful friends, Bob Jenkins, he "busted his ass" his entire life. And later, when I was old enough, I busted mine trying to keep up with him. As a boy, Dad and his brothers worked in the fields picking peas with the Mexicans at the San Diego farms south of Victor. He cut firewood for a few bucks a cord. He bucked hay. Later he worked teams of horses dragging logs out of the mountains for local lumber yards. He built trails in the mountains for the Forest Service. He trained and shoed horses, milked cows, thrashed grain, irrigated potatoes and built fences. When I got old enough I often accompanied Dad on firewood cutting outings or cutting posts and poles that he sold to local farmers and ranchers. He was handy with a chainsaw and never seemed to lack for work.

Mom was a Utah girl, the youngest of fourteen children born to Peter Herman Lott and Fernie Annette Moore. She was born in Joseph, Sevier County, Utah, but remembered nothing of Joseph because her family moved to Fielding, near Tremonton, when she was a tiny baby. I remember a saying my Mom joked about that she learned from her older brothers and sisters. She said: "My Dad was a Lott, but my Mom was Moore." Grandma Fernie died when Mom was only three months old, so Mom didn't remember her. Grandpa remarried and had four more children with his second wife. So, besides her thirteen full brothers and sisters, Mom grew up with three step sisters and one step brother. All together, Mom had seventeen brothers and sisters.

Mom's life as a youngster mirrored that of Dad's. She worked in the fields thinning sugar beets and leading the derrick horse during hay stacking time. One day when she was nine she was climbing in a tree, lost her balance and fell, breaking her left arm in the process. This was problematic because she was a total southpaw. It was a bad break. Upon seeing it, Grandpa twisted and jerked her arm to reset the bone, then told her to go into the house and lie on it. That was the extent of her medical treatment, but she was tough as a desert lizard and I imagine she bounced back quickly. The set wasn't exactly perfect, and years later you could see how it had healed crookedly, but she had full range of motion and no problems using it. When playing sandlot baseball with us years later in our Victor pasture she could make the throw from home to second without any problem. As I recall, few of us stole second on her.

When Mom completed high school at Bear River High in Tremonton in 1950, she journeyed north by bus from Fielding to Victor to help her older sister, Vernessa, who was about to have a baby. Aunt Vernessa was married to a fellow named Joe Winegar at the time. Joe and Dad were friends and that's how Jerry Jones and Fern Lott met.

Dad never said this, but Mom told us kids a little about their courtship. She said after they met, Dad often would come to the house, ostensibly to see Joe. He would knock and Mom would run to answer the door and Dad would say: "Is Joe here?" Mom liked telling us this story because it embarrassed Dad. Other than that, neither Mom nor Dad ever said a whole lot about their romance, but I'm sure it was steamy because they both were very passionate. Neither hid emotions well. I've heard some couples claim after thirty years of marriage they could never remember saying a cross word to one another. That would not have been my Mom and Dad. Neither of them ever would have said anything that ridiculous because if one would have said it the other would have called "bullshit" immediately.

However, though they never pulled any punches verbally, there never was a physical altercation of a hostile sort that I ever saw. And their verbal jousts most often ended with a smooching session on the couch in the living room. In fact, Mom and Dad were very affectionate toward one another. When Dad came home from work he would wrap his big long arms around her and hug and kiss her. I liked seeing that. As a child I always felt warm and peaceful when they showed their affection for each other. All of this easily explains me and my brothers and sisters. I was the oldest. Kenny was next, then Cathy, Tommy, Nile and Annie.

Our family lived peaceably amongst our neighbors and friends for the most part. We didn't have much, if any, money in the bank, but we didn't have any skeletons in our closets either, unless you count the moose that was in our freezer.

A DOLLAR AND A LOT OF LOVE

Dad's older brother, Gordon, owned an acre of ground shaped like a triangle north across the road from his house in Victor. According to the deed, he sold it to my Dad for "a dollar and a lot of love" in the early nineteen fifties. It made one of those mortgages that can never be paid off entirely. The dollar was paid at the time, but I don't think we ever gave enough love to pay for that little piece of rocky ground. As I look back over the decades that have passed since then I can see there couldn't have been a better place for me to grow up.

Dad bought a little house from the Weekes brothers and moved it onto the acre. Over the years as our family grew, Dad and Mom added a large living room with a basement under it. It never was too big and we kids always shared beds and bedrooms, but it was warm and it was home.

About the time I was born, Dad took a job working at the Nelson-Ricks Creamery in Victor, which bought milk from local dairymen and made cheese. Back then, most farmers had a dairy herd and counted on the milk check for regular income. A friend of Dad's, Blaine Boyle, operated the creamery. Dad worked many years at the creamery and when he left, I worked there one summer when I was fourteen before the creamery closed down.

My little brother Kenny was my main playmate through these years. We slept in the same bed for years. Tom and Nile also shared a bed. When Ken and I got too big to occupy the same bed comfortably, we swapped out brothers. Tom slept with Ken and Nile with me or vice versa. We were flexible. Cathy and Annie also shared a bed when we were young. Then one day Dad brought home some bunk beds and solved the sleeping problem.

Kenny and I both were born with club feet. His were worse than mine. My feet were corrected with casts but Ken's required an operation. He had big stitch lines along the side of his feet he liked to show off. I envied his stitches back then. After we started to walk we got along fine and never gave our feet a second thought. We could run, walk and do anything that our cousins and friends could, the only difference being that our feet were flat as two-by-fours.

When I started first grade, Kenny got bored without me and took up the craft of making airplanes from kindling wood. Using a hatchet in the shed, he chopped small pieces of wood from larger blocks. We learned how to do this because we had a wood stove to keep us warm in the winters and we watched Mom and Dad do it all the time. After chopping a few sticks, he would pound a nail through two pieces of wood to make a cross which served very well as a toy airplane. This was done without Mom's knowledge and you can almost guess the result.

One day while I was at school, he chopped off his right index finger at the bottom of the finger nail. Mom threw him and the end of his finger in the car and sped to the hospital in Driggs where Aunt Ada, a licensed practical nurse at Doctor Kitchener Head's office, sewed it back on and put a bandage on it. The doctor was out of town at the time. The finger healed pretty well, but looked a bit odd. Aunt Ada was rightfully proud of her stitching job. Most people with a wound like that lose the finger. Kenny was happy to have an end on his finger.

A few days after he lopped his finger off, Kenny pulled the bandage off to show me the stitches. It was bloody and gooey so he let the dog and cat lick it to clean it up. That must have felt good to him because he did that often until it healed. It sort of grossed Mom out though and whenever he did it she got upset with him and chewed him out while she rebandaged it.

Kenny often called me "big brother." I liked him to acknowledge me as the "big brother" and he knew it, so whenever he had a bone to pick with me and he didn't want the discussion to disintegrate into fisticuffs, he would say something like "Big Brother, you're a pain in the butt" because if he acknowledged my big brotherness and then insulted me, he most often got away with it. He also called Tom and Nile "Little brothers" and Cathy and Anne "Little Sisters" with or without the insults.

After a while, Cathy, Tom, Nile and Anne picked

up on the "big brother" salutation and began to add their own insults. Cathy, Tom and Nile would usually say something like "Hey big brother, fat butt" and then they'd run as fast as they could because I would chase them with a broom. It got to be kind of a game and eventually a term of endearment because one time Anne climbed into my lap when I was watching television. I was about fourteen or fifteen so that would have made her four or five. Anyway, she sat on my lap and snuggled in, putting her head on my shoulder. Then she said: "Big brother, you're a pain in the butt" and hugged me.

Kenny always was asking me random questions. Because I was the "big brother" I was the expert on all subjects. The topics were wide and varied, but usually involved my death in some horrific fashion, like "Russ, would you rather be run over by a milk truck, a snow plow or a school bus?" These questions very often would result in some sort of argument. I learned to never answer the question directly because it just encouraged him to ask more.

Here's an example of how our conversations went:

"Russ, which would you rather be eaten by, a grizzly, a wolf or a mountain lion?"

I'd say something like: "I'd shoot all three of the sons of bitches."

"I didn't ask you that," Kenny would say. "I want to know which one you would like to be eaten by."

"I don't want to be eaten by any of them," I'd respond. "That's why I'd shoot them."

"We're not talking about shooting them," he said, sighing. "I want to know which one you'd rather be eaten by, a grizzly, a wolf or a mountain lion? Will you please answer the damn question?"

"A crocodile," I'd say. This type of circular conversation was typical and would normally end up in a wrestling match with us on the floor laughing or we would bloody each other's noses and Mom and Dad would make us sit in the corner for a while to cool off.

Ken never was naïve. He was always explaining things to me that I should have been explaining to him. I think it was because he played with our cousin Bo so much. Bo's older brothers, Leonard, Jerry and Richard, all served in the U.S. Navy. Somehow he learned stuff and taught me stuff, mainly words and songs, I never would have dreamed on my own. I won't share any of that here because I hope my children and grandchildren will read this and I am already pushing the outside of the envelope with some of my words. One morning I sang one of the songs Bo taught us that he learned from his older brothers. Dad said: "Where in the shit did he learn filth like that?"

Kenny also was more socially outgoing than I was. When we got older I remember a time when he and I were walking along Main Street in Victor, probably after baseball practice. We saw two young women walking toward us. I don't know how old they were, but they were both several years older than we were. One was rather pretty and the other a little on the homely side. Ken wanted to talk to them. I didn't. I was afraid of any girl who was not a relation. I would freeze up and be unable to think of anything to say. It was so bad for a time that Ken nicknamed me Kalijah after the wooden Indian in the Charly Pride song.

Anyway, he tried to convince me that we should talk to them.

"This will be good practice for you Russ," he said. "I'll talk to the cute one and you can try to convince the other one to go to the beauty parlor."

OH MY HELL!!

While Kenny and I were learning to navigate through the problematic feelings that girls always seemed to cause, we were oblivious to the trials and challenges of our younger sister Cathy.

Cathy had to be tough or die. Looking back I feel bad for the way we treated her sometimes. She was sandwiched between two older callous, insensitive brothers and two equally rough-and-tumble younger brothers before Annie came along. There wasn't a lot of girl-type stuff that went on in our house. We were centered on horses, guns, fishing, hunting and sports. Her two older brothers, Ken and I, weren't warm and fuzzy. Mom protected her as much as possible, but when Mom was out of sight we didn't cut Cathy much slack.

As a result Cathy developed a mental and emotional strength superior to anything the rest of us had. I can't explain it easily. It may be that it was innate. The first time I really noticed it was on Pioneer Day--I think about nineteen fifty-eight. Our ward primary organized a parade and we all were supposed to dress up as pioneers and walk up and down Victor's Main Street. With a white sheet, Mom fashioned our red wagon into a miniature covered wagon. She put a seat on the front and placed Cathy on it. Cathy was old enough to sit but not walk all the way. She wasn't quite two. Mom dressed her in a little pioneer dress with a bonnet. Kenny and I were the horses. Tom was still a baby so he stayed with Mom. The parade started out and everything was just fine, but parades start and stop a lot and sometimes the starts are a bit jerky. As Kenny and I jerked the wagon along the parade route, Cathy toppled over backward and sat there clinging to the sides of the wagon with the cover collapsed hanging on for dear life.

    We were too little and goofy to care if she was sitting up or not so we carelessly kept going. I remember looking back at her and seeing an odd look on her face as she clung to that wagon trying not to fall. At the time I didn't know what that look meant. Now I do. Her eyes were round and wide with terror, but she didn't make a peep. She was true pioneer stock and it was appropriate that it was Pioneer Day. She didn't laugh; she didn't cry. We paraded all the way down Victor's Main Street until we turned around and walked all the way back, Cathy toppled over backward and silently clinging to the wagon afraid she might fall off. When Mom saw us she rushed over and said: "How long has she been like that? Why didn't you sit her up?"

    I replied: "Mom, she didn't cry or say anything."

    Mom nearly yelled at me: "She never does."

    A few years later, after she learned to talk fairly well, Cathy developed her signature cusswords. I remember the first time very well. Kenny came running into the house breathless and excited. Mom was in the kitchen and I was watching television.

"Mom, come quick," Kenny said. "Cathy's swearing like a sailor."

We all went running outside. Cathy was standing in the front yard with her arms folded and head down, very ashamed. Her bottom lip was sticking out and she was about to cry. She had mud on her dress. Tom and Nile were standing close by, eyes big as silver dollars. Annie was crawling around on the lawn, still a little small to understand what was happening.

I should say here that we, Cathy's brothers, exposed her to a lot of barnyard language we picked up from our U.S. Navy-trained cousins. We truly could cuss like sailors, at least Ken and I could and we taught Tom and Nile, but only when we were out of Mom's hearing. Mom let slip an occasional bad word when she was mad. Dad had moments where he could blister all oxygen molecules within a thirty-yard radius. But for Cathy to cuss was unnatural and a big concern to Mom because she wanted at least one of her kids to have some class.

"What did you say?" Mom asked in her quiet voice. Cathy kept her head down and didn't reply. Mom looked at Kenny and asked again. "What did she say? It's okay. You can tell me and you won't get in trouble."

Kenny wasn't bashful at all.

"We were making mud pies. Nile's broke and he threw it at Cathy and it got on her dress and she said 'OH MY HELL.'"

Mom looked around at all of us, rolled her eyes and scooped Cathy up and took her into the house. We don't know what was said, but Ken and I later decided that Mom must have given Cathy special permission to cuss because from then on Cathy said "oh my Hell" a lot. It became her signature cussword and she uses it to this day.

As Cathy grew older she had no problem expressing herself. Like Mom, she developed a biting wit mixed with extraordinary amounts of sarcasm and cynicism. And like Mom, she never was without a comeback comment to anything we said or did. At that point she didn't show us any mercy either and she could rip any one of us to shreds with an offhand comment about our cowlicks, pimples or poor color coordination. It was the one weapon she had to defend herself and she knew how to use it.

One night in my teenage years I got ready to go to a Saturday night dance at the stake center. These were common especially in the summer. I spent an hour hogging the bathroom bathing, shaving, combing and applying Aqua Velva.

When I came strutting out of the bathroom into the kitchen, Cathy was standing in the kitchen doorway and looked me over carefully, then closed her eyes and shook her head in a pitying way. She would have been twelve or thirteen then.

"What?" I said. I wanted to yell at her, but Mom was sitting in the kitchen corner with her nose in her Anatomy and Physiology textbook. This was during her college years so she was always studying. I wanted to escape without raising her ire so I toned it down. Since I asked the question, Cathy was happy to answer.

"Big brother, you have a big pimple under your left nostril, your cowlick is standing at attention and, oh my hell, someone has to teach you that the only place it's legal to wear white socks is while you're playing basketball."

About that exact moment Kenny walked into the kitchen right in the middle of this conversation. He piled on.

"Big brother," he said, sniffing and making a face. "You smell just like a French harlot."

Now I know that Kenny had no experience whatsoever with French harlots. To that point in his life he'd rarely even been out of eastern Idaho. He probably didn't even know what a harlot was. His comment, undoubtedly, was something he picked up from Bo and our U.S. Navy-trained cousins. Mom lowered her book and I could tell from my vast experience that Kenny was about to catch Hell and I was happy be a witness. Her glasses were sitting on the end of her nose like a librarian would wear them. Until that second I don't think Kenny even knew she was there or he would not have made that comment.

"Kenneth Jones," she said sternly. "Sit down in that chair and tell me everything you know about French harlots."

Kenny sat down with terror in his eyes. For some reason it was very satisfying to me to see him embarrassed and speechless because he was never embarrassed or speechless. I smugly patted him on the back and thanked him for the diversion. I escaped and went to the dance with my pimple, cowlick and white socks. I smelled good.

Cathy was the smartest of all of us; she always got good grades in school. After she learned to read she constantly had her nose in a book or had one in her hand or under her arm. That wasn't unusual for our family, however, we all read because there wasn't much else to do in the winter when the snow was drifted up to the window sills. Did I mention we only had one TV channel then? At one time I could recite the program lineup by heart. Most of us read Jack London, Zane Grey and Louis L'Amour novels, Cathy took it to a whole new level reading Jane Austin, Herman Melville and Charles Dickens and other exotic authors. She didn't mess much with *Riders of the Purple Sage* and she read in the summertime too. She and Nile even read encyclopedias and other reference books. I don't know if it was because of superior intelligence or incredible boredom. Whatever it was, the rest of us never were afflicted with it.

SONS OF BITTIES AND SURLY BADGERS

I have cousins on my Mom's side of the family I never have met and wouldn't know if I saw them on the street even though Mom taught us the names of all her brothers and sisters, our aunts and uncles, and their children. With the exception of Aunt Vernessa and her children, we never saw them enough to really know them like we did our Jones cousins.

Mom told us stories about Grandpa Lott and her stepmother she called Aunt Nettie and that her ancestors were Mormon pioneers who were among the first settlers in the Salt Lake Valley. She even knew some of her pioneer family names like Cornelius Peter Lott and John Smylie Lott.

We never officially had family home evenings. As Mom put it, "the lesson book was a little too spiritually advanced for us." Dad often listened quietly as Mom taught us about church and family members. One night Mom told us about Cornelius, her great, great grandfather. Now most Mormons don't brag if their great, great, great grandfathers were Danite generals, but mine was so I won't gloss over that part because it kind of goes along with my narrative. According to some of the historical records I've read, he not only was a churchgoer, but he knew how to cuss too. As Mom told us about Cornelius that evening, Dad looked at me and I could see he was itching to say something so I continued to stare at him until he moved his lips. It took me a minute but I finally got the main idea. Kenny saw it too.

"Mean sons of bitties," his lips said as he shook his head gravely. Usually Dad didn't edit his words into church-approved language, but he toned it down in the house around Mom. Dad was a reader of western novels and other like materials and came across the Lott family name in connection with early Missouri and Utah events in some of his readings, and he liked to tease Mom about some of the things he read. Mom's ancestors, Cornelius and John Smylie Lott, were polygamists; Dad brought it up often when he wanted to tease Mom. Polygamy was a sore spot with her, like it is with most Mormon women, and she didn't like being reminded of it. Truth be known, Dad's teasing was a compliment because he'd met Mom's brothers and he knew them to be as gnarly as he was. That's how we complimented each other; we teased. Dad often said stuff like this to get a rise out of Mom, because she always was ready with a comeback. Anyway, when he whispered "mean sons of bitties," Mom saw it and read his lips. Her eyes narrowed and she gave him a withering look. If looks could kill, Dad would have been lying on the floor dead as a moose. But she didn't let on to us that she was peeved, at least not for a few seconds.

"Yes children," she said, sweetly acknowledging

Dad's silent comment. "Your Lott ancestors were a little rough around the edges, but infinitely more refined than your Jones ancestors who were surly baaaa....ddgers."

Mom also used church-approved language around us kids when she was calm or trying to remain calm. Dad slapped his knee and roared. He couldn't stop laughing for about a minute. Then he grabbed Mom and gave her a big hug and kiss after which they sent us kids to bed and had a smootchfest on the couch.

When we hit the bedroom, Tom and Nile had a bunch of questions.

"What the heck is a surly badger?"

They were a little confused about the conversation that had taken place. They missed the lip-reading part and didn't know that "surly badger" was a surrogate term that Mom made up on the spot to protect our youthful purity, naivete and innocence. Kenny, as usual, was quick with the interpretation. He hadn't missed a thing. So, he explained.

"Dad said Mom's ancestors were mean sons of bitches, and Mom said Dad's ancestors were surly bastards," he said. "That's about the size of it."

"Are they mad at each other?" Nile said.

"No," Ken said. "Didn't you see them kissing on the couch?"

Then he patiently explained to Nile and Tom one of the secret truths about the Jones family.

"For some reason, there are times when it's hard for us Joneses to say 'I love you' to each other. We're a prideful bunch so it seems a little clumsy and gooey to us. Instead, we call each other mean sons of bitches and surly bastards."

We all thought about that for a while. Finally, Nile said: "So if Mom's ancestors were mean sons of bitches and Dad's were surly bastards, what does that make us?"

Kenny sat down on the bed next to Nile and put his arm around him in a big brotherly sort of way so he could break the news to Nile as gently as possible.

"You, little brother, are a full-blooded mean son of a bitch and surly bastard," he said. And so am I, as are Tom and Russ."

"Which is worse? Or better?" Tom asked.

"Doesn't matter. We're both," Kenny answered.

"What about Cathy and Annie," Tom kept on. "Which are they?"

"They're just like us," Kenny said. "Except they're girls and you don't call girls mean sons of bitches and surly bastards and if you ever hear somebody call them that you beat the hell out of them and if you're not big enough you come and get Russ or me and if we're not big enough, then . . ." He paused here thinking and we all pictured in our minds the escalation of a conflagration with all the surly bastards and mean sons of bitches in the family coming down on some poor miscreant who had misspoken.

"Get the picture?" Kenny said. "This is a family thing. Nobody outside the family gets to call us mean sons of bitches and surly bastards because it doesn't mean the same thing when they say it. Understand?"

Tom nodded: "Got it. Except I don't think we need to protect Cathy and Annie. Maybe they could protect us."

Nile wanted to know what I thought: "Russ, which do you think you are?"

"I don't know," I said, being my usual evasive self. "I think I am equal amounts of both."

"I think you and Nile are surly sons of bitches," Ken said.

"Then you and Tom are mean bastards," I retorted.

"I can live with that," he said.

"Me too," Tom said.

"Me too," Nile said.

That being settled, we all ducked under the covers and went to sleep.

I should give our ancestry a little more context right here. Mom's great, great grandfather, Cornelius Peter Lott, made quite a name for himself in early LDS church history. He served as a Danite general who led raids on the Missouri mob usually to uncover hidden caches of weapons during the Mormon war of eighteen thirty-eight. The Danites were church members who organized to protect themselves from the depredations of the Missouri mob. The pukes, the name the early Mormons gave to Missourians because they drank whiskey, chewed tobacco and stunk, claimed Cornelius and the other Danites were killers. The Mormons claimed they didn't kill anyone and the Danites were doing nothing more than defending themselves and their families.

Later, when the church was located in Nauvoo, Cornelius served as the captain of Joseph Smith's bodyguard. He was an exceptionally good man and while living in Nauvoo was the superintendent of Smith's farm and spent many days helping build the Nauvoo temple. He liked to carry around a wicked-looking blacksnake bullwhip and is said to have been the only man to have beaten Joseph Smith in a wrestling match.

Whatever Dad read described Cornelius as a mean son of a bitch so Dad got a kick out of repeating it because it always made Mom flinch. Cornelius was a close friend and next door neighbor to Joseph Smith and was the father of one of Joseph's numerous wives. Cornelius collected a passel of wives himself. Unfortunately, despite all of his church service, the main thing he is remembered for in church history is that he was a captain in the Heber C. Kimball company that crossed the plains to Utah in eighteen forty-eight, and he made the mistake of telling Mary Fielding Smith, one of Hyrum Smith's widows, not to cross the plains until she was better prepared. Sister Smith did not take kindly to his counsel and, according to the story told by her son Joseph F. Smith, crossed the plains despite Cornelius, enduring his daily scorn and humiliation.

Sister Smith ultimately won this little feud because Joseph F. Smith, later became church president and memorialized his contempt for Cornelius. Since there's no one in our family tree who rises to the stature of Joseph F. Smith, we pretty much have to concede that Cornelius, in addition to being a polygamizing Danite, must have been surly and mean. Joseph F. Smith may never have called Cornelius a mean son of a bitch, but as the years have passed the terms Cornelius Peter Lott and mean son of a bitch have become synonymous in church history. He ranks right alongside his contemporaries and (probably close friends) John D. Lee and Orrin Porter Rockwell. With Dad's interpretation of this story and others about Cornelius, it's not a stretch to see how we, and others, came to think of Mom's antecedents as mean sons of bitches.

Dad's ancestry was a mystery to us at the time of this particular family conversation. I should add a little history about the Joneses here just to balance things out. On the Jones side, the contemporary of Mom's ancestor, Cornelius Peter Lott, was a man named James Naylor Jones. He also was a Mormon and he and Cornelius probably knew each other. James also served as one of

Joseph Smith's body guards, and later in Nauvoo suffered an attack by a mob where his house was burned and his milk cow stolen. There is no record of any retaliation, but knowing the Joneses the way I do, I suspect that house and milk cow came out of somebody's hide. Mom would have been delighted to know that this one of Dad's ancestors also accumulated a large collection of wives, came across the plains only one year after Cornelius and was the first white man to winter among the Indians in the Fairview, Utah area. He lived a life every bit as colorful as Cornelius. She could have used that information to her advantage in her verbal jousts with Dad. Oh, what could have been. Thankfully, Mom didn't know this, because she would have used that knowledge in a way that only Mom could have, and in that scenario, a divorce might have ensued.

    I need to introduce a concept here that most people don't seem to know. It's a practice the early Mormon settlers in the Great Lake Salt Valley used with great effectiveness. It's called vermin hunting. When they first arrived in the valley they had difficulty with predatory animals getting into their livestock and causing other problems. Thousands of dollars worth of grain and livestock were destroyed by the vermin. John D. Lee called them "wasters and destroyers." The vermin were wolves, wildcats or catamounts (bobcat or lynx), polecats (skunks), mink, bear, panthers (cougars), eagles, hawks, owls, crow, ravens and magpies. Brigham Young named John D. Lee and John Pack as captains to rid the area of these animals. The captains decided to have a competition so they chose up sides so there were two teams of one hundred men each. Cornelius was on Lee's team. A raven wing was worth one point. Owl, hawk and magpie wings were worth two points; eagle wings five; polecat and mink five; wolf, fox, wildcat or catamount skins were worth ten; and bears and panthers fifty. More on vermin hunting in a minute.

My Dad never knew his grandfather, Joshua Oliver Jones, who died about ten years before Dad was born. But he did know that Joshua came from southern Utah. One of the things he didn't know, or at least never mentioned, was that Joshua was the only son of James Naylor Jones and his second wife (first plural wife) Mary Haskins Childs. They divorced soon after Joshua was born in 1853, but I use this lineage to claim that I, and all descendants of Joshua Oliver Jones, are genetic Mormons. In other words, we would not exist if the early Mormons had not practiced plural marriage. All of my Dad's brothers, and most of his uncles were big athletic men, over six feet tall, and while they are polite and affable gentlemen, you don't want to see their surly side. Trust me on this.

Our Jones progenitors moved into the Teton Basin during the summer of eighteen ninety-five. Great

Grandpa Joshua was something of a nomad. He was born in Lehi, Utah, then lived in Panguitch. After marrying Susan Maria Elmer, they moved to Brigham City, Arizona, where he tried farming a few years before moving back to Utah where they lived for a time in Cannonville and Escalante. Finally he came north into Idaho where he homesteaded some land just west of the present-day Victor town site. He had a good team of mules and made his living as a freighter. My grandfather Elmer Jones was born in Victor in November of that first year. He was the seventh of ten. Soon thereafter Grandma Susan announced she wasn't moving any more, either because she liked Victor a lot or because she was tired of traveling so much. So they stayed even though life was hard.

    Like all settlers, they farmed and lived off the land.

    The Joneses had their own style of vermin hunting. Joshua and his sons were largely responsible for wiping out the grizzlies and wolves in Teton Valley during the early nineteen hundreds. Our family diet consisted of deer, elk and moose which is basically the same diet as grizzlies and wolves, which ate far more than their share, so we either shot them or trapped them. By the mid-thirties these vermin were mostly gone with a few stragglers remaining, but even the stragglers soon learned to move on or get a bullet in the head. By the time I and my brothers and sisters and cousins were born in the 1950s, the grizzlies had retreated into Yellowstone Park, about thirty miles to the north and there were no wolves.

That suited us just fine.

With the wolves and grizzlies gone, big game of the antlered variety did very well in the mountains surrounding Victor. Their numbers increased and they thrived through most of the Twentieth Century. I should mention here that grizzlies and wolves of the early Twentieth Century were a nuisance, not the angelic and gentle creatures that environmentalists and oxymorons worship today. I'm not saying the Joneses killed all the grizzlies and wolves around Victor. There were other ranchers and farmers in and around Victor who didn't care for the vermin either and I'm sure they killed some too, but the distinction of being the one most responsible for administering the final coup de grace to the grizzlies and wolves has to go to the surliest bastard of them all, my grandpa, Elmer Jones.

Grandpa Elmer grew up wild. In the early nineteen hundreds, Victor was still the wild frontier. There were no stores or emergency services beyond your neighbors. Self reliance was pre-eminent.

When he was old enough, Grandpa got himself a Winchester 32.40, Model 1894, one of the first non black powder rifles ever made. He became an excellent marksman. My dad, himself an expert rifleman, later told me he could not shoot anywhere near as well as grandpa could with that 32.40. The 32.40 wasn't a big gun, but it was big enough for grandpa, who was fond of saying "it's not how much lead you put in the air; it's where you put it." The 32.40 had a long barrel and was accurate over several hundred yards, at least for an expert like Grandpa.

Grandpa hunted, trapped, farmed and made a living on the farm west of Victor. In nineteen seventeen, he married his sweetheart, Irene Barnhart. By most accounts, to that point he was a fairly normal human being. He and Irene had two children, Gordon and Dale. The thing that turned Grandpa Elmer into a certifiable surly bastard was malevolent and horrible. It's one of those things that happen to all families at some point in some form. And it's one of those things that make you ask "why did this have to happen?" and then you question God and you never hear an answer you want to hear. It makes some people humble. And it makes some people surly bastards.

In the winters of nineteen seventeen, eighteen and nineteen, a great flu epidemic swept across the world. By some counts up to forty million died in the United States alone. Among them were Elmer's wife Irene and his youngest son, Dale. I don't know what Grandpa felt. Like all of us, he was complex individual. I'm sure he felt a profound sadness and grief. And if he was anything like me, one of his grandsons, he felt frustration, helplessness and anger. He may have felt dangerous to be around, or maybe he just wanted to get away. Whatever the reason, he left his remaining son, my Uncle Gordon, with his mother, saddled his horse, loaded his 32.40, packed a few supplies, mainly the largest bottle of whiskey he could find and disappeared in the mountains south of Victor in search of the main things he knew needed killing. About a week later he emerged with a pack horse loaded with grizzly and wolf pelts, sold them, reloaded his gun and bottle, kicked a few asses at the Timberline and disappeared again into the mountains. He repeated this process many times over the next several years. It's called surly bastard therapy.

After several years of therapy, grandpa re-entered society. In nineteen twenty-five, he married Eva Jemmett, a pretty young woman from Shelley, and over the next twenty-one years fathered my dad and aunts and uncles. In order of birth they were Joyce, Mel, Dad (Jerry), Faye, Jewell, Connie, Ted, Boyd, twins Blaine and Brent, and Randy.

Grandpa apparently had a personality like a porcupine. My Dad loved him and that's the way it should have been. Grandpa died in nineteen fifty-three of a massive stroke/heart attack, about a year after I was born. My mom later told me that it's a good thing for our family that grandpa died when he did because she could not have remained married to my dad "because grandpa was so ornery." Mom probably meant that Grandpa was hard to love and that maybe he could have used a few more years of therapy.

A few years after Grandpa died, Grandma Eva moved her children who still lived at home to Firth, a little town between Shelley and Blackfoot, where she would be closer to her mother and other members of the Jemmett family. She never remarried.

AN ADDED MEASURE OF SURLINESS

Moose eater number four in the family was Tom. His full name was Thomas Elmer Jones, after grandpa. I'm not sure if that gave him an added measure of surliness or not. He was five years younger than me.

As a little boy of about eighteen months, Tom got tonsillitis and an ear infection. The infection actually damaged his hearing and he still suffers from it. One morning when he was about three, he came to the breakfast table with a big green gob of snot oozing down his upper lip from his nose. He either didn't care or was unaware of it as he ate his corn flakes. Ken, seated on the other side of the table, silently stared at him for the longest time without saying anything.

Finally, Kenny couldn't stand it any more.

"You gonna eat that lamb chop or can Russ have it?"

Normally, it took more than that to make me groan, but it was one ugly, and unappetizing, lamb chop. Usually I didn't take it upon myself to wipe Tom's nose, but somebody had to do it and the commotion brought it to Mom's attention and she washed Tom face after I had smeared it around a little.

I suspect that Tom and Nile had the same sort of relationship that Ken and I did. They fought like dogs and cats. When they were in the seven, eight or nine-year-old range, Kenny and I decided it was time to teach them how to play football. We had learned at school and both of us enjoyed it because it was the one activity where you could hit somebody as hard as you wanted and not get in trouble for it. Even though there were a few years difference in their ages, Tom and Nile always were about the same size so we figured it would be a fair match if Nile was on my team and Tom on Ken's.

Nile and I had the ball first so I hiked the ball to Nile and playfully blocked Kenny who played along because after all this was just to show our little brothers how the game was played. Tommy's job was to tackle Nile. Tom laid Nile out like Dick Butkus on a quarterback. It was brutal and text book, shoulder planted in gut, arms around legs and drive the ball carrier backward. Ken and I suddenly realized we weren't teaching a pair of girls to play tag. Our little brothers already knew a lot more than we thought and obviously liked contact too. In addition, they might have had some issues.

The two of them got up and brushed off, trading deadly looks. Kenny and I traded looks too. We didn't have pads or helmets and this looked serious. We knew we had to shorten the game.

"Okay," Kenny said. "Our turn to have the ball."

Kenny hiked to Tom who took off full blast for the end zone. He probably had a better idea what was coming that we did. It was like instant replay. Kenny and

I didn't even fake a block. We just stood and watched. The exact same thing happened with the only difference being that Tom was the quarterback and Nile was Dick Butkus.

We picked them up, brushed them both off, congratulated them on how fast they were catching on and pronounced the game over before one of them got killed. At that point they both were shooting fire out their eyes at each other. So we all went inside and Ken and I tried to get them interested in a game of Monopoly.

Tom was very athletic, but he didn't seem to be that interested in sports. For a few years he played on Victor's Little League team with Nile. He was the pitcher and did extremely well, but he liked other things more-- horses, hunting, fishing and girls. He had about the same interest in school as Ken and I did.

From a young age, Tommy was very interested in medieval and Native American weaponry—spears, bows and arrows, hatchets or tomahawks. Later, he got interested in black powder rifles and put one together from a kit he ordered through a catalog. At one point Tom contemplated the construction of a Roman-style catapult. That was the result of a road apple fight he got the worst of when Nile and I ambushed him and Kenny near the corral on our place and then hid behind the haystack. Tom got a little bit cross about it and threatened to bury us under a hundred pounds of horse crap he planned to launch from a catapult. The catapult he envisioned was huge and probably would have thrown three hundreds pounds of horse dung three hundred yards which would have buried Nile and me forever. I think we could have talked him into turning it around and launching it from our pasture into Victor's Main Street, which would have become legendary in Victor annals, but it didn't happen because Dad used Tom's raw materials to build a buck fence. Actually, they were Dad's raw materials that Tom was using to build the catapult, but Dad beat him to the punch and built the buck fence before Tom could build his catapult.

Tom blazed his own trails and did not necessarily mimic anyone else. He won the Explorer Olympics in archery two separate times in Idaho Falls with a bow he made himself. He made saddles, tanned hides and was more of a cowboy than any of us. As a teenager he worked for Uncle Jewel putting up hay and wrangling cows on a ranch near Jackson. He took lessons in Driggs to learn how to fly small aircraft and, after high school, studied in Pocatello to become a fixed-wing aircraft mechanic. He's pretty smart and very handy. Today, if he doesn't know how to do something he learns how by watching videos on YouTube.

"You can learn how to do anything on YouTube," he says.

If someone told me today that my little brother Tom

was building a sailboat, or an airplane, or both, in which he was planning to circumnavigate the globe, it wouldn't surprise me in the least.

HISTORY REPEATING ITSELF

    To the west of our house about a hundred yards at the end of the lane, lived the Mayor of Victor, Floyd Stratton. Not only was Floyd the mayor, but he was also in the Victor Ward bishopric and was school bus driver and custodian of Victor Elementary School. He was very visible in our lives. His daughter, Susan, was playmates with Cathy and cousins Betty and Ava.

    Between Uncle Gordon's place and Stratton's was about an acre of land with a little, unoccupied house on it, surrounded by apple trees and lilac bushes. We called this place Violet's because it was owned by a lady named Violet. I never met Violet; I never saw her and I don't know where she lived. Uncle Gordon knew her because he irrigated the pasture, kept the fence up and his horses grazed the pasture in the summers. This house and place was unoccupied all the years when I was growing up and Violet's place was a favorite place to play for me, my brothers and sisters and my cousins.

    Floyd had a street light situated on the edge of his and Violet's property. The light was on a lone-standing pole about fifteen to twenty feet high. A two hundred-watt bulb shed light on his yard and driveway. It was covered by a tin shield that looked sort of like a hat and which covered the long neck of the bulb but the main orb on the bulb hung below the shield. I never really paid any attention to this light until I was about eight years old. That was the year that Kenny and I got Daisy Red Ryder BB guns for Christmas.

Our BB guns came with strict rules. Do not shoot, or even point, these guns at anyone, especially little brothers and sisters. Do not shoot at windows. Do not shoot your eye out. Mom was the enforcer and she was tough. I learned that the first month. Outside in sub-zero weather with snow up to my butt, I was trying to find a target when I spied the snow plow. A man on a tractor with a snow blade was clearing our road from the droppings of the most recent blizzard. He was seventy-five yards away, far out of my BB gun's range, but I lifted my gun and trained my sights on the big wheel of the tractor. I don't think I fired a shot, but Mom saw me from the living room window. I lost my BB gun privileges for a month.

Most inanimate objects were okay to shoot—rocks, posts, tin cans and cardboard boxes. In real cold weather, Dad would get a cardboard box and draw a target on it and then stuff it with old rags or towels and on a few occasions Dad would let us shoot in the living room. We could shoot a package of BBs into the box and then retrieve the BBs which we thought was a pretty good deal.

When summer arrived, we got a whole new set of

targets, mainly birds. Starlings, black birds, magpies and crows were okay to shoot, but we learned that if we shot at robins, they better be the ones eating Mom's strawberries. Once we had cleared the robins from the strawberry patch, we got a little bored and started to range farther from the house looking for new quarry.

One evening at dusk, Kenny and I spotted the perfect target. We were at Violet's circling a lilac bush looking for birds when it jumped out at us—about 40 yards away, hanging there in the sky was Floyd's 200-watt yard light just begging to be shot at.

"I could hit that," Kenny said.

"No you can't," I said. "It's too far away."

"Watch," he said. He lay down on his stomach and drew a bead on that light. He took a deep breath and then let it out like Dad taught us. Pffft. The BB arched across the field and hit the tin shield. Ping!!! The ping was really loud so we hunkered down behind the lilacs and waited to see if anyone stirred. No one did.

"You hit about two inches too high," I said.

"Okay," Kenny said. He took aim again. Pffft. Ping!!! He hit the shield again.

"All right," I said. "It's my turn." I lay down on my stomach like Kenny had and took careful aim. The bulb seemed to be getting bigger and brighter by the second. I took a deep breath, let it out and squeezed the trigger. Pffft. POP!!!

The "pop" scared the crap out of us. We scurried back through the bushes to the fence, where we looked around to see if anyone was out and about. No one. So we hurried across the road and into our house where we nonchalantly put our guns under the bed.

The consequences weren't too severe. If Mom and Dad had found out we probably both would have gotten switched with a willow and lost our guns to boot. That happened on occasion. I remember once after Kenny and I had our butts switched, sitting on our bed and commiserating.

"They'll get easier to live with and nicer as they get older," Kenny said.

"I don't see that happening," I said. "They'll be switching my butt when I'm thirty years old."

We didn't lose our guns for a month for shooting the yard light because, apparently, Mom and Dad never found out. Floyd did not alert Mom and Dad, but he did catch us out in the field the next day and told us if we ever did it again he'd make sure we lost our BB guns forever. So, that was the last time Kenny and I shot at Floyd's street light, but, as it turns out, it wasn't the last time his light got popped.

About five years later, Tom and Nile got Daisy Red Ryder BB guns for Christmas and history repeated itself. In Tom's words, this is what happened:

"I imagined wading through snow in Kentucky with

Daniel Boone. About dark, I was in deep, dense forest (Violet's backyard). Rounding a big boulder (Violet's house), I saw the biggest buck in the world (Floyd Stratton's street light). It just double-dog dared me to shoot it and no one can resist a double-dog dare. I took careful aim, steadying against the boulder, and squeezed off a shot. It was like watching in slow motion and ten-power magnification as the BB arched its way straight to that light. I heard the "pop" and the light went out. I thought 'OH MY HELL, what do I do now?' I thought if I backtracked and got out of there fast, no one would be the wiser. But, a day or two later the axe fell. Mom asked Nile and me who the shooter was.

"'Not me.'

"'I don't know.'

"Our guns were taken away forever, or until the culprit spoke up. I knew Nile did not fire the shot. He wasn't even there with me. I couldn't let his gun get taken away for what I did, so I fessed up. Got my gun grounded for a month."

That wasn't the only time Tom had his BB gun grounded. There was the time he shot Nile in the back.

"I thought I was dead," Tom recalls. "He came after me and I ran straight to Mom saying Nile was going to shoot me."

That's when Mom learned Tom had already shot Nile. The guns were grounded again.

Apparently, Tom and Nile shooting each other with the BB guns got to be a habit and they would have wars with each other. The summer I got home from my mission I remember standing in the doorway between the kitchen and living room. Tom and Nile would have been sixteen and fourteen, respectively, at that time. Tom came busting through from the bedroom and nearly knocked me down. Nile was right behind him giving chase. Tom almost got to the porch when Nile shot him right in the butt.

Mom was standing right beside me watching. I looked at her and she just shrugged.

"Since I went on my mission, discipline around this place has just gone into the toilet," I said. "You need to cut a willow and blister both their butts because that's exactly what you would have done to Kenny and me had we behaved that way."

She laughed and said something like: "I'll have your Dad do it. I'm easier to live with and nicer than I used to be."

SEEING THINGS AND HEARING THINGS

Moose eater number five was Vernile Paul Jones. He was two years younger than Tom. We called him Nile. As a little boy Nile learned to drive as soon as he could walk. That's what he did, all the time. Anything that was round, he would use as a steering wheel, a plate, a can lid, a hula hoop, a piece of paper he cut in a circle, you get the idea—all he needed was the steering wheel. He supplied the engine, the engine noise, screeching brakes and tight corners. He drove everywhere he went, up to the corner, around the pasture, over to Uncle Gordon's or to Aunt Vernessa's, while walking down the railroad tracks, from the bedroom to the living room, from the kitchen to the bathroom. He drove. In the wintertime, he drove us all crazy with his driving because it was constant. The sound effects were free.

For a few years, Dad had a Ford Mercury parked behind the house where the garage is now. The engine was ruined in it and Dad planned to replace the engine at some point when he got enough money. Eventually he sold it to Clifford Barker, but at the time it was a great playhouse for us kids. We all played in it, but no one got more enjoyment out of it than Nile, who drove it around the world several times I'm sure without it moving an inch. He could turn corners, shift gears, stomp on the gas and apply the brakes. If Nile came up missing we almost always could find him with Wayne, Jimmy and Annie, heading off to California in the Mercury.

One summer day, Tom and Nile were playing in the Mercury. As usual, Nile was driving and got low on gas and pulled into the gas station. Tom was the station attendant. Nile told Tom to "fill 'er up," and so Tom filled it up using the garden hose turned on full blast. Kenny and Bo saw it about the time the tank filled up and dressed Tom down.

"Dad's going to beat you black and blue," Ken told Tom, and Bo poured it on too telling Tom that Dad was going to kick his butt so hard he wouldn't be able to walk for the rest of the summer. Anyway, after ten minutes of that type of scolding Tom decided he needed to find a new place to live so when he heard somebody say "Dad's home," he split. He started running out past the haystack and shed, down along the railroad tracks to the end of the line and out into the tall grass of Schiers' big field.

Thus began the search for Tom, the fugitive. Cathy walked down the tracks calling for Tom, but he didn't reveal himself even though he could see and hear her from his hiding spot in the grass. He also could hear Mom whistling and calling for him. When Cathy went back to the house, Tom rose up and ran farther away toward the creek. Tom was on the lam for about an hour and was walking upstream along Tonks Canal toward

Trail Creek when he was spotted by the posse, consisting of Kenny, Bo and Gary Matkin. Bo let out a war whoop and they soon surrounded Tom, whose legs were still a little short and stubby to outrun them. The posse dragged Tom back to the house to face the inquisitor, no doubt reminding him of the torture he was about to experience. I think they were expecting to get some sort of reward, but all Dad did was laugh big guffaws and hug Tom, who was still bawling, and expecting to be executed at any moment.

When Nile started school, he brought home playmates after school and they always played in the old Mercury. One of his playmates was a little girl named Wendy Johannson. Mom and Dad were friends with Wendy's parents so they often visited and Nile and Wendy would play for hours in the Mercury. It's a memory I find especially heartwarming. I don't know why, but Cathy, Tom and Ann remember it too. The Johannsons moved not long after that and I have no idea where they went.

Nile was often preoccupied and the older he got, the more preoccupied he became. If you ask what he was preoccupied with, I have to say I don't know. It was odd. One morning Mom watched as Nile headed out the door for school. He was in the second or third grade and nearly late that day, but didn't seem concerned or worried by the way he walked up the road. I was home that morning and watched Mom watching him. Nile would stop and pick up a rock and examine it closely before proceeding.

"What's he doing?" she said. At the corner where a trail was worn through the sagebrush toward the school, he stopped and stared at a piece of sagebrush for the longest time.

"I wish I knew what was going on in that kid's mind," Mom said. "He's got his own schedule and he just won't be hurried."

Nile did very well in school. He was extremely intelligent and I often wondered if he was contemplating some huge cosmic problem he ran across in one of his textbooks. Years later he opened up to me and told me he saw and heard things he didn't think other people saw or heard. That was heavy. We didn't know this when he was in high school. Sometimes he seemed a little weird and distant, but what teenager doesn't seem weird and distant?

Nile had a severely dry sense of humor. While hunting with cousins Vern, Roy and Larry one time, Nile jumped up some deer. When he met up with the cousins for lunch he mentioned the deer.

Larry asked: "What were they?" meaning were they bucks or does?

Nile's response: "They were mule deer. What the hell other kind of deer is there?"

They still laugh about that. I should mention here that we loved hunting with our Driggs cousins. They were the happiest bunch of guys you ever will see and very good hunting companions. They always were laughing. I wondered at the time if they were laughing at us or with us. But it didn't matter. They were family and it was always fun.

Nile's sport was baseball. When Tom got too old to play Little League, Nile took over the pitching duties on Victor's team. Until then he had been Tom's catcher. He excelled. When he was a Little Leaguer, he could throw a ball nearly as hard and fast as I could and I was seven years older than him and a pretty good player if I do say so myself.

During Nile's last year playing Little League, Victor was playing a team from Driggs that had a big, tall pitcher who, like Nile, was a flame thrower. The game was in Victor and was a game of strikeouts. The Driggs pitcher would strike out the Victor batters, and then Nile would strike out the Driggs batters. The game was decided when Nile was batting. He turned on one of those fastballs and lifted it over the left fielder's head. Victor didn't have an outfield fence so the ball just kept going after it hit the ground and bounced all the way to the Victor church, where it hit the back wall and bounced back about ten feet.

I remember thinking that if Nile could get the right

coaching and the right opportunity, he could maybe someday play pro ball. But that was wishful thinking. Baseball opportunities are few and far between in Teton Valley where snow is on the ground eight months of the year. The only one who really ever might have come close was Uncle Gordon, whose baseball hopes ended during the Battle of the Bulge in World War II with an arm wound. Nile's baseball dream never even got a good start because he had other demons to fight.

    The summer I got home from my mission Kenny, Tom, Nile and I all played on the Victor Ward men's softball team. Tom and Nile were still in high school, but we needed some players to fill out our roster and they were as good as any of the rest of us even though Nile was only fourteen and Tom sixteen. The first game I was playing third and Nile was playing left field when one of the opposing players hit a ball over my head and deep, down the left field line just fair. It was an easy double for the guy but he was thinking triple. He saw we had a fourteen-year-old kid playing left and decided to take advantage. Nile got to the ball about the time this guy rounded second and tried to stretch his hit into a triple. There was not a man on that field who could have made the throw Nile did. I didn't have to move my glove to catch it and if I would have moved my glove I probably would have missed it. It was like a streak of light. When the runner got to third I'd been waiting for him for the longest time with the ball in my glove and a big smile on my face. That was one of the most satisfying tags I ever made during a ballgame because I heard that guy say one of those words you're never supposed to hear in church ball, but so often do. The word got around that summer. Nile was a player.

When Mom started working as a nurse at the Teton Valley Hospital, she often would work the swing shift and because it was such a small hospital most of the time she was the only nurse on duty. One night about 9 p.m., a woman brought her son to the emergency room. He looked like he'd been in a car wreck. He had numerous bruises and cuts on his face. Mom called Dr. Head who soon arrived and began to stitch the patient up. Dr. Head was a gregarious and inquisitive man and he started asking questions.

"What happened to you?" he asked the kid.

The kid didn't want to talk but after some questioning he finally admitted he'd been in a fight. The doctor laughed. He often was called on to clean up such messes.

"Where's the other guy?" he asked. There's usually two of you needing a few stitches."

"Don't know," the kid said. He didn't want to talk.

Doc Head went on with his jovial banter.

"Well, what's his name? Maybe we should send the ambulance for him."

The kid said nothing, but his mother, who obviously didn't know who Mom was, piped in about then.

"It was Vernile Jones," she said. "He's a mean little son of a bitch."

The doctor got a big kick out of that, but didn't rat Mom out. He grinned at her and kept up his happy banter until the woman and her son left. When Mom got home that night she checked Nile out. He had some skinned-up knuckles, but otherwise he was okay. We never found out what the fight was about.

The older Nile got the less communicative he became. He grunted a lot and answered direct questions, but you had to pry information out of him. During high school he lost interest in sports and kept to himself a lot. His behavior bewildered me. I know Mom and Dad wondered and worried about him.

The spring he graduated from high school, he and Mom went to Idaho Falls. Mom had some sort of training meeting at the hospital there and while she was in her meeting, Nile killed a few hours doing his thing. A few months later we found out what that was. While Mom was in her meeting, Nile enlisted in the U.S. Army. He let Mom and Dad in on it a few days before he left for basic training. Mom was extremely frustrated that he hadn't at least discussed it with her.

"Why is he so surly?" she asked me one time as if I was the resident expert on surliness.

Years later, Nile told me about some of the things he saw and heard. When he was in high school one time he was sitting in the car in front of the Teton Valley Hospital waiting for Mom to finish her shift as a nurse. At that time the hospital had numerous landscaping boulders in front between the parking lot and the main building. As he waited, he saw a couple of these large rocks rise off the ground and hover in the air in front of the car.

"I thought that was a little odd," he said. He tried to describe other things to me that he saw, but had difficulty finding the right words. I could see it frustrated him to try to explain these occurrences to me so I stopped pressing him although he volunteered once that he had seen the devil at a bus station in Dillon, Montana.

"What did he look like?" I asked.

"He was dressed like a huckster," he said. "Nice suit, tie, hat and he had a load of money stuffed in his pockets."

"How did you know it was the devil?" I asked.

"Because he dragged a twenty-foot tail onto his bus and nobody blinked an eye."

MORE LIKE FIONA THAN SNOW WHITE

The last of the moose eaters is Annie. As I've already mentioned while telling you about Cathy, it was a huge disadvantage being a girl in our house. Our lives took place mostly outdoors even in winter. We rode horses, shot guns, played baseball, football and basketball, hunted and fished, not traditional girl activities, although Annie got pretty good at some of them. We came home to eat and sleep and sometimes watch television. Did I mention we only had one channel to watch, KID-TV in Idaho Falls? After a few years, an NBC affiliate began broadcasting, KIFI, also in Idaho Falls. Our favorite shows were Red Skelton and Gunsmoke.

During inclement weather, which Victor has its share of, particularly during the winter, we, of necessity, had to come indoors and that's when the house got a little small. The older we got the smaller it got. Being the smallest and least experienced, Annie had a distinct disadvantage. She never fell for the snipe hunting thing, but she spent an hour one morning going through the cooking utensils looking for a bacon stretcher. One day Ken sent her to find a left-handed fork and spoon for him. When she couldn't find them, she asked Cathy who educated her pronto.

One of the things we learned as children was how

to build fires. We had a wood stove which had to be lit each morning so we knew how to cut kindling, wad newspaper or paper bags and strike matches. Sometime in the sixties we got a Stokamatic which burned coal and would hold a fire all night long. Dad would bring a load of coal home, dump it into the basement through the coal chute. We would haul the coal up from the basement in five-gallon buckets and dump it into the Stokamatic which had a small electric auger in it to feed the fire. This created another chore of taking the coal clinkers outside daily.

But even the Stokamatic sometimes went out and we had to build a fire, basically the same process as starting a fire in the wood stove. We also had a burn barrel out in the backyard for burning excess paper and cardboard garbage.

One day when she was three or four years old and all the rest of us were at school. Mom told Annie to clean her room. While doing this little chore she built up a nice stack of paper she had to dispose of. She decided to burn it, but skipped the step in the process of taking the paper to the burn barrel. She lit them right in her and Cathy's room. After igniting the paper, she realized she was in trouble so after trying to blow out the flames and failing, she stepped out of her room and closed the door.

Dad was still working at the Nelson-Ricks Creamery in those days and about that time he arrived home for lunch. Annie starting coaxing Dad to take her for a ride, but he declined because he really didn't have time. But she knew she had to get Mom and Dad out of the house so she continued coaxing right up until he and Mom smelled smoke. They opened the bedroom door to find the room in flames. Luckily, they caught it in time and after a few frantic moments of firefighting succeeded in putting it out.

They then had to find Annie, who had hidden behind the Stokamatic during the panic, and was fearful that she might have to go to prison. When we got home from school that night we all admired Annie's handiwork. There was a big black scar in the girls' room that went from the linoleum up the wall to the ceiling and we all got a lesson in being careful with fire.

Annie came home from school one day when she was in second grade and told Mom she was dropping out of school because she did not want to be anything when she grew up so there was no point in her studying any more. I'll give you a hint who won this battle—ten years later Annie graduated from high school.

I have difficulty describing Annie as a tomboy because she is so gentle and kind, never eschewed domestic duties or chores and was every bit as feminine as Mom and Cathy. She was not as interested in books as Cathy, but then, who was?

From a very early age, she loved all animals, dogs,

cats, horses, pigs, chickens, and so on. Like all of us she loved to watch wildlife. I remember her spanking her cat, Patches, when she killed birds, but I don't think she cared about the mice and gophers so much.

She spent a goodly portion of each summer climbing apple trees at Violet's going after the little green apples that grew there abundantly each summer.

I can picture Annie in my mind skipping around through the forest like Snow White or Cinderella with the birds singing and lighting on her shoulder and hand, while she kneels down and pets the squirrels and the bunnies and the skunks. Deer follow her around and all the forest creatures love her because they sense she would never do a thing to harm or scare them.

On the other hand, Annie wore jeans most of time, rode the horses bareback and sometimes without a bridle, spit on sidewalks and got into as many fights as her brothers did. So in that regard she was a little more like Fiona than Snow White.

MOOSE-EATING COUSINS

We had several families of moose-eating cousins to mix with too. Across the railroad tracks to the north of our place, on the mean son of a bitch side of the family, lived my Aunt Vernessa. She was a lovely, grandmotherly woman. Her first marriage to Joe Winegar ended in divorce, but she never moved from her little spot in Victor.

Aunt Vernessa had pansies and petunias all over her yard whenever it was warm enough for them. She also had plum trees and a big raspberry patch, rhubarb, and about everything else that would grow in Victor. Every year she had a huge garden where she tried to grow a little of everything, but what usually happened in Victor is the string beans, peas, radishes, onions and potatoes would grow just fine and she'd get a good harvest, but the corn and tomatoes would freeze. Aunt Vernessa and Mom and Dad loved corn and they would try every year to grow some. Almost never happened, but every year they tried. One year I remember Mom and Dad getting a few ears of sweet corn from our garden.

Aunt Vernessa's children included Leonard, Jerry, JoAnn, Richard, Diana and Larene from her first marriage. Leonard, Jerry and Richard were the sailors. All went into the Navy during the fifties and early sixties. They all were five to 10 years older than me so we didn't do much together, but I knew who they were and they boxed my ears from time to time. Diana and Larene were closer in age.

When Aunt Vernessa divorced from Joe Winegar, she married Vearl Weekes, Uncle Doad. He and Aunt Vernessa had one child, Vearl David Weekes. We called him Bo. Bo was a wiry little rascal. He could climb any tree and he and Kenny would give chase to any wild thing with four legs, even skunks, but especially rabbits and ground squirrels. They were the Jack Russell terriers of our neighborhood. Bo was like another brother. As we grew up he hunted, fished and camped with us. We were at home at his house and he was at home with us. We didn't have any secrets from each other, but that's the nice thing about cousins, you don't have to explain about the missing moose, because they helped eat them.

Bo always had special kinds of pets like rabbits, hamsters and chickens. One spring Bo caught a baby duck in Tonks Canal, which we called the crick. He took the duck home and raised it in a cage. Another year, his dad brought home some baby crows that they raised in the same cage. When the crows, Squawk and Caw Caw, learned to fly, they liked to torment Mom whenever she walked through the pasture to visit Aunt Vernessa. The crows would fly about ten feet above Mom and swoop down at her. They never touched her but they always made her cuss and all of us laugh. Mom was very happy when they finally flew away and never came back.

Bo and Kenny were the same age so they spent plenty of time together and sometimes they'd let me play and boss them. We rode horses, shot our BB guns, caught grasshoppers, dug worms, fished and played war. While playing war, you need weapons, mainly guns and grenades. Any board or stick works for a gun, but rocks were too hard for grenades when we were little so we avoided throwing them at each other. But we had horses that left plenty of piles around the pasture. When these piles of road apples dried they made fine grenades so we pitched them at each other from dawn to dusk. Sometimes, when the battle escalated into a nuclear confrontation, we pitched the fresh ones.

Other weapons were bows and arrows. A green willow with a piece of twine worked well and would sling a green willow arrow up to 10-15 feet. We also made flipper crotches aka sling shots. Flippers require the fork of a tree branch about eight inches long with a narrow piece of tubing from a car or bike tire, plus a leather tongue from an old shoe. Dad made these for us because construction required a sharp knife and precision. We never killed anything with them, but not for lack of trying. Our dogs and cats were our main targets.

Bo's dad raised hogs. They had several hog sheds and a low-voltage electric fence that surrounded their place to keep the pigs in. The fence consisted of a single wire about 12 to 14 inches off the ground which the alternating current pulsed through. The wire was held up by small posts with a white insulator the size and shape of a spool of thread. Even as little boys, we easily could step over it. You just had to make sure not to touch the wire. Even if you did, at most you got a small shock and then you learned to be more careful. It was very effective at keeping the pigs penned.

One day Bo asked if I would like to join his and Kenny's club. I don't know how old we were. I was probably seven or eight and Bo and Kenny six or so.

"Sure," I said. "I want to be in your club."

"There's an initiation," Kenny said. "Here. Drink all of this."

He handed me an old military canteen filled with water. I was a little wary, but the water tasted okay, so I drank it. They then blindfolded me and led me out behind Bo's place. There was a shed around an old sawmill near the electric fence. They led me behind it where no one could see us.

"What's the name of this club?" I asked.

"The Pee Kings," Bo said.

I knew about this club and I was already a member and I said so. This was a club where we had contests to see who could make the highest mark on the side of the shed.

"This is a new club," Kenny said.

"With new by-laws," Bo said. "You have to perform one simple task. You have to pee on the electric fence."

"Why?" I asked suspiciously.

"It will cause sparks and fireworks," Bo said. "It's really cool looking."

Everybody loves fireworks, even me. Kenny pointed to the white insulator on a nearby post.

"Just hit that and you will see things you've never seen before and you will be an official member of the Pee Kings."

That seemed like something that was well within my range of abilities. I looked around to make sure no one else was watching and then I hit the insulator with a full stream. That's how I learned that water is an excellent conductor of electricity. It was just low voltage, but the jolt knocked me on my butt and I hollered. Bo and Ken headed for the house laughing all the way. As soon as I composed myself I went looking for them, but they had hidden and I couldn't find them the rest of the afternoon.

At least once a year Aunt Marge and her children drove up from Salt Lake City to visit. Aunt Marge's kids included twins Frank and Floyd, Little Margie and Linda. When they came it was a party and when they went home, I always wanted to go with them and I'd cry when Mom pulled me out of their car as they left.

Aunt Vernessa worked for a long time at the Dutch

Oven Chicken eatery next to Pierre's Playhouse in Victor. Like Mom, she was an excellent cook. Mom probably learned a lot of cooking skills from Aunt Vernessa. She was about 13 years older than Mom and was as much a mother to Mom as a grandma to us.

Music was extremely important to both Aunt Vernessa and Mom. They loved to sing. Aunt Vernessa had a little organ at her house that she played, but most of the time they sang A cappella. Whenever they got together they would sing and their voices blended beautifully. They sang church hymns, popular music and all sorts of folk songs.

When I was a boy, Mom taught me to sing. She sang around the house and she had a beautiful voice. I liked it when she sang. I remember some of the songs she taught me: *Faith, Hope and Charity, You Are My Sunshine and Mr. Sandman*. Those and many others.

Aunt Vernessa's daughters, Larene and Diana, sang with Mom and Aunt Vernessa sometimes and for a few years the four of them competed as a quartet at the Teton Stake Talent show. I think they won two years in a row and were in high demand for funeral numbers for quite a while after that.

In August of nineteen seventy-three, a few months after returning from my mission, the phone rang at our house about 1:30 in the morning. I answered it. I learned then that calls in the middle of the night usually are not good news. It was Bishop LaMar Thompson. He told me, as kindly as he could, that my cousin Bo had been in a car accident near the white bridge south of Driggs and had been killed. He asked me to tell Mom and meet him at Aunt Vernessa's. It was a shock. It was horrible. Bo was only nineteen. There was nothing to do but go visit Aunt Vernessa and try to comfort her. She ended up comforting me.

Aunt Vernessa handled the news better than I did. Mom described her as a rock. She was a strong, steady woman. We all loved Bo, but Bo's death didn't seem to surprise Aunt Vernessa. She had seen a lot in her life. Her mom and many of her older brothers and sisters died young so she was familiar with hardship and picking up the pieces after a family death. She allowed herself to cry some, but then she looked up, hugged me and Mom, composed herself and took care of business. If she cried anymore, it was when she was all alone where no one else could see.

She died a few years later of a heart attack at the age of 60. To me she seemed older than that. She had been admitted to the Teton Valley Hospital and the doctor decided to transport her to Idaho Falls for more specialized care one morning. Mom was not working at the hospital that morning and when she learned Aunt Vernessa was being transported asked that the ambulance stop in Victor so she could help with Aunt

Vernessa's care on the way to Idaho Falls. Aunt Vernessa died about the time the ambulance got to Victor. It was March eighteenth, nineteen seventy-eight.

Across the street to the south, on the surly bastard side of the family, lived Uncle Gordon, Aunt Ada and their children Irene, Linda, Trina, Ava, Betty, Wayne and Jimmy. Except for an occasional game of baseball, Irene, Linda and Trina usually were not interested in playing, which was okay because they were older and had other fish to fry. Ava and Betty were game for most anything from climbing apple trees to hide 'n seek, tag and road apple fights. Irene, Linda or Trina sometimes babysat us on Saturday nights when Mom and Dad went to Snowballs in Swan Valley to kick up their heels.

Uncle Gordon was Teton County Sheriff for several years when Kenny and I were teenagers. One night, he needed to talk to Dad and could see activity in our basement. We had an outside entrance to the basement so Uncle Gordon walked down the steps. A few seconds later he walked back up the steps, muttering under his breath: "I didn't see anything. I didn't see anything."

What he didn't see was Dad, Del Matkin and Dee Humble skinning a moose.

Like all my Dad's brothers, Uncle Gordon was a superb horseman and always was game for a horseback ride somewhere. He owned several horses and almost every year traded for or purchased a new one. He, like

Dad, loved to race cutters or chariots, so some of his horses were more than just saddle horses. One of them was an appaloosa, a big-boned gray gelding with a few spots on its hind quarters. Its name was Appie. Appie was a big, gentle horse, very good with inexperienced riders.

Wayne was about the same age as Tom and Nile. I think he was a year younger than Tom and a year older than Nile. When Wayne was little, Uncle Gordon wasn't ready to turn him loose on a full-sized horse no matter how gentle it was, so he purchased a Shetland pony, a little pinto, for Wayne to learn on. This presented several problems. The first problem was that the pony was not trained. It was young and had to be broken to ride. The second problem was that all the adults were far too big to ride this size of a pony, so they couldn't train it. It was even too small for Betty and Ava. The only ones the right size to ride it were Wayne, Jimmy, Cathy, Tom, Nile and Annie. Uncle Gordon came up with an ingenious solution.

Since the pony wasn't much bigger than a good-sized sheep, riding it wasn't any more dangerous than mutton-busting so he fixed it up with a bridle, led it to the corner of the pasture farthest from the barn, placed Wayne on it and turned it loose. It bucked all the way back to the barn, depositing Wayne about halfway. Then he gave all the kids a turn. The kids rode that little pinto all summer long taking turns. They did exactly what Uncle Gordon showed them. They led the horse to the far corner of the pasture and whoever's turn it was got on. The horse bucked back to the barn usually depositing the rider somewhere along the way. They all got bucked off numerous times. It was hilarious to watch. I think they were disappointed when it stopped bucking. Before the summer was over that little pinto was trained to ride and Wayne and Jimmy had themselves a very good saddle horse and they and their cousins knew a lot about training a young horse to ride.

Uncle Gordon was a superb athlete. In high school he competed at the state level in track and field. He also played other sports in high school, basketball, football and especially baseball. Dad told me stories about Uncle Gordon's baseball abilities and that he might have played pro ball after the war if he hadn't been wounded at the Battle of the Bulge. But stories are only stories until you see for yourself.

When I was fourteen I fancied myself a baseball pitcher. One afternoon Kenny and I were playing catch on the front lawn and Uncle Gordon walked across the street and wondered if he could show us a few things. We were hungry for coaching so Uncle Gordon and I started playing catch. Near as I can figure, Uncle Gordon would have been about 50 years old then. He hadn't played ball for many years and the old war wound would have been a hindrance. He threw easily for a few minutes as he loosened up and then the balls started coming a little harder and faster. I should mention here that both Kenny and I were not bad baseball players. We could catch about anything thrown at us by kids our own age and older. I played shortstop and third base at Teton High and Kenny played catcher, but as I mentioned, Teton didn't have a top notch baseball program then and our coaching was haphazard at best.

As Uncle Gordon continued to throw faster and faster, the balls started doing interesting things as they came at me, things I had never seen before. At times they would hop. Other times they would seem to rise the last few feet before they hit my glove. He warned me before he threw a ball that cut to my left (inside to a right handed batter). Then he threw a changeup, with the same motion as if it was a fastball, but it was like he had the ball attached to a string and the ball seemed to slow down and I could hear the backspin as the seams cut the air and then spun in my mitt.

Then he started throwing some curves explaining to us that a pitcher can get along without a curveball, if he can locate his fastball and changeup wherever he wants. He threw several overhand curveballs that would break anywhere from eighteen to twenty-four inches. After throwing one of those he said:

"I never could throw a good curveball overhand," he

said. "My best curveball was underhand."

"What?" I said.

"Watch," he said.

He threw the next ball underhand, like a fast pitch softball pitcher. It came toward my left shoulder where I had my glove positioned to catch it, and then it broke to my right. It was a hard, sharp break and it just kept going. The ball changed directions. I dived to my right but still missed it. He laughed.

"You have to know when those are coming and where they're going or you'll never catch them."

Sometimes I have tried to imagine what it would have been like if Uncle Gordon hadn't been wounded and if he had made it to the big leagues. A life that could have been, a different life. He and Aunt Ada probably wouldn't have come back to Victor to live so then we wouldn't have really known them. I don't like that scenario.

One of the saddest things to happen in those years was Wayne's accident. Looking back, I think Wayne must have been the spitting image of his father. As a little boy he was athletic in the extreme. He was good at everything, running, throwing, he could do everything with ease.

Once the little pinto pony was broken to ride, he rode it everywhere and soon became an expert horseman, maybe a little too good. He was fearless and he soon outgrew the little pinto and started putting his saddle on Appie. It was sort of a funny sight to see him sometimes with his little saddle on that great big horse, but he could handle Appie with ease and, like the pinto, he rode him everywhere. At the time Wayne was eight, Tom was nine, and Nile was seven.

One day he and Tom were galloping along the Cedron road when Wayne's cinch slipped and his saddle fell sideways. The Cedron road in those days was a gravel surface. When Wayne fell, the impact crushed his skull and he nearly died. After weeks in the hospital, he came home, but he had brain damage and was permanently disabled. He never totally regained the use of his limbs, especially on his left side, and he had to learn how to walk and talk again. In my mind it was a feat every bit as difficult as becoming an Olympian.

Eight miles to the north, in the township of Driggs, also from the surly bastard side of the family lived Uncle Mel, Aunt Ellen and their four boys—Rod, Vern, Larry and Roy. They matched up in age pretty close to me, Ken, Tom and Nile. They were the absolute best hunting companions because they understood the Jones family hunting philosophy which had been passed down since Grandpa Joshua entered Teton Valley in the 1890s. The philosophy basically says that "all big game is fair game placed on this earth by God for our use. All grizzlies and wolves should be shot on sight, but never shoot an animal you don't intend to eat because it's a terrible sin to shoot an animal and leave it. And, half the fun of hunting is outwitting the game warden."

My cousins always made me laugh whenever I was with them with their Jones style hunting humor. They still do. One time I was hunting with Roy. Roy is a No. 1, topnotch tracker, far better than me. Roy is such a good tracker that when he sees a herd of elk he doesn't just jump off his horse and shoot one. He'll herd the whole bunch down the mountain closer to his brother, Larry, whom Roy calls Lawrence. Don't ask me why. Lawrence isn't as good a tracker as Roy but is a better shot although there seems to be a dispute between them over who's best.

One time, Roy and I were following an exceptionally large elk track. We hadn't seen the elk, and we didn't know anything about it except that it made very large tracks. The track took us through some steep country with a lot of down timber. Suddenly, Roy stopped and got off his horse. He had found a pile of droppings. He picked up a piece of elk dropping, holding it between his thumb and finger. He squinted at it for a few seconds. Then he rolled it around in his palm. Finally he gave it a squeeze and threw it back down onto the ground.

I watched the whole thing closely, waiting patiently for his analysis. Then he got back onto his horse and was about to ride on when I said, "Wait a minute." I had sat through the entire ritual and I wanted to know what he had learned. Roy turned sideways in his saddle and motioned for me to ride closer. He whispered.

"It's a bull. He weighs about 750 pounds and is about 10 minutes ahead of us and moving fast. His rack has six points on one side and seven on the other. He's a little lame in the left hind foot because of a cougar attack when he was a calf, but he sure has a nice set of teeth."

A less experienced hunter would have to taste elk droppings to get that much detailed information. But that's not as sporting.

We kept following that elk until it was almost dark. That's when we saw him. He was lying down curled up like a puppy in a warm corner. Horns were poking out all over the place.

He saw us about the same time we saw him and came out of his bed in one jump. We both slid off our horses and started blazing away. That's how I learned why Roy likes to herd the elk toward Lawrence.

Like his brothers, Vern also is a fair shot with a rifle. If an elk is standing broadside within fifty yards and isn't moving, Vern can drill it right through the liver.

Uncle Mel was Driggs city marshal for many years. He was the city's main law enforcement officer, but his job entailed a lot of maintenance work as well. I never saw him carry a gun, unless we were going hunting with him. After all, it was Driggs. Nothing too exciting had occurred since 1832 at the original Pierre's Hole Rendezvous when some trappers and a Blackfeet war party shot each other up.

Now, you might be thinking that you don't believe much of the stuff that I am writing. That's okay. I do have a tendency to embellish and I may have a tendency to overstate how big and strong and athletic my uncles and Dad were. To me, they were bigger than life, no more so than on August twenty-seventh, nineteen seventy-one, when then Driggs City Marshall Mel Jones was called on to investigate a shooting east of Driggs. It turned out that three young migrant workers had been murdered by a man named Michael Rennpage. He intended to steal their vehicle. His plan was derailed because he couldn't get the boys' vehicle to start after he killed them, giving their younger brother, who Rennpage wounded and left for dead, a chance to escape and get help. The younger brother returned to the scene with Uncle Mel, who brought Dr. Head with him to try to help the boys who had been shot.

When Uncle Mel arrived at the scene, the first thing that happened was Rennpage shot him in the chest with a .38 revolver. The second thing that happened was Uncle Mel jumped on him, took the gun away from him and then subdued him by fracturing Rennpage's skull with it. I always thought Uncle Mel was a real gentleman for his restraint. No one in this world, and probably not in heaven either, would have objected if he had taken that gun and blown the top of Rennpage's head off. Instead, he simply gave Rennpage a nice little concussion and let the law do the rest of the work. Rennpage later was convicted on three counts of second-degree murder.

We nearly lost Uncle Mel that August, but after spending weeks in an Idaho Falls hospital, he recovered and is still alive today. I was on my mission when this happened and I thought about it a lot. I've wondered if I ever took a .38 slug in the chest would I survive? Did Uncle Mel survive because he was tougher than boiled owl poop? Or, did the Lord protect him? I'm inclined to believe that he had angels round about that night who helped him. And if that's the case maybe we should rethink a lot of things we assume about the Jones family. Then again, I'm sappy that way. I like to believe things like that. And I like to embellish so I'm going with the angel theory even though in our family story there are a number of times that it didn't appear that the angels were anywhere nearby.

Uncle Jewell was the proverbial boy named Sue. To me, he was like a great big teddy bear whenever he came to visit. Like all my Dad's brothers, he was good natured and polite. One time he gave me a fishing pole just because he had an extra one, but apparently, like all the Jones uncles, he had a surly side that I never saw.

Russell Jones

When I was fourteen I worked one summer at the Nelson Ricks Creamery in Victor after Dad no longer worked there. Dad was a friend of Don Boyle, who ran the creamery then. Sterling Cherry worked there too and also was a good friend of Dad's. In the afternoons we'd sit outside during break after the curds had been stuffed in the canisters and put on the rack and Don and Sterling sometimes would tell me stories about my Dad and uncles.

They were good stories. The one I remember best was about Uncle Jewell, who as a boy had problems with some of his school mates. I like to think they were teasing him about his name, Jewell, but I don't know. Dad already had told me stories about when they were kids and Uncle Jewell would come home after school with his shirt ripped to shreds from being in fights. Dad said the fights were usually against two or more and Uncle Jewell usually got the worst of it, at first. But with practice, combined with heavy dose of Jones surliness, he got so he could handle multiple opponents. Don corroborated and reinforced that story. He said Uncle Jewell most often would walk home from school past the creamery and often as he walked past a group of four or five boys (we'll say five because I like to embellish) were nipping at his heels, calling him names, pushing, shoving and so forth. Uncle Jewell took it. Blaine Boyle, Don's father, was managing the creamery then and watched this go on for several days.

"Finally," Don said, "My Dad stepped outside and called out to Jewell and said 'don't let them do that to you. Kick their asses.'"

Apparently, all Uncle Jewell needed was a little encouragement because he waded into them. After that, they left him alone. That apparently happened many times throughout his life. Once his tormenters got a dose of his fists, they left him alone.

"Jewell could get those big fists of his going like a couple of jackhammers," Don said. "I never wanted to be on the receiving end of those fists."

After Uncle Jewell married Aunt Pat, their family lived in Jackson. They had four children, Terri, Donna, Casey and Brett, and they came to play sometimes.

Dad and Uncle Jewell were the same height, but Uncle Jewell was stockier than Dad. Dad never was much heavier than 180 and he looked sort of skinny. But, like their brothers, they were really strong men.

I remember Dad and Uncle Jewell shoed a lot of horses together especially in the springtime as the dude ranches around Jackson and Wilson were getting their horses ready for the summer. One day, when Dad had a day off from the creamery, he took me, Kenny, Tom and Nile along on a horseshoeing job and Uncle Jewell brought Terri and Donna. They had about nine horses to shoe that day near Wilson and we ran around outside the corral as they worked. After a couple hours they had shoed eight of the nine horses. The only one left was a big roan gelding that was kind of wild. They had to rope it and it wouldn't let them touch its feet. So finally they put it on the ground by trussing it up with ropes around its hind legs. It was the first time I had ever seen that done, but within a few minutes they had that horse tied up like a pig so that it couldn't move its legs, but it still thrashed it head around.

Dad called to me and told me to sit on the horse's head and pull its ear. Once I sat down on its head and neck and started twisting its ear, the horse didn't move and within about twenty minutes Dad and Uncle Jewell had it shoed.

Despite all the trouble that horse was to shoe, both Dad and Uncle Jewell liked it and said they wished they owned it because it was big, sturdy, and they judged with some training it would be an excellent saddle horse. I think they felt a kinship to that horse because it was a lot like them.

Shoeing horses is dangerous work and Dad shoed hundreds of them over the years and so did his brothers. Once a horse kicked him and broke his wrist as he was shoeing it. Another time he got so mad at a horse that he kicked it and broke his toe. And he always had cuts usually from horses jerking their hooves when he was nailing the shoes on. Sometimes the cuts were so bad he had to get stitches. When I was a kid, the going rate for shoeing a horse was six dollars. Except for shoeing his own horses, Dad quit shoeing horses sometime in his forties because it was back-breaking work and the pay wasn't worth the aggravation.

HE WAS WILLIE, I WAS SANDY

When my mother was a teen-ager, the Lott family farm was in a little town in northern Utah called Fielding. I find it ironic that part of our family lived in a town named Fielding given Cornelius's feud with Mary Fielding Smith almost one hundred years earlier. When Mom was a teenager television had not arrived in the Lott home yet, and radio was the main source of entertainment. Mom liked baseball and listened to Brooklyn Dodger games broadcast by Red Barber and later, Vin Scully. The Dodgers had a pretty good team and almost every year went to the World Series. The problem was that every year the New York Yankees went to the World Series too. And every year the Yankees broke her heart.

My Mom was a fan of the underdog in almost every case. She married my Dad in nineteen fifty-one when the Dodgers still had not won a World Series. She stuck with the Dodgers and when I and television came along I kept her company whenever there was a Dodger game on TV. The Dodgers finally won the World Series in nineteen fifty-five against the hated Yankees and then again in nineteen fifty-nine against the White Sox. It didn't really register in nineteen fifty-five because I was only three, and in nineteen fifty-nine I didn't care because they played the White Sox. To me it wasn't a real World Series unless the Dodgers were playing the most obnoxious team in baseball, the Yankees.

    The Dodgers had an interesting player, a second baseman, who was the ultimate underdog. Jackie Robinson was the first black player ever to play Major League baseball and became a national icon during his playing years. My Mom taught me all about baseball, Jackie Robinson, Roy Campanella, Johnny Podres, Don Newcombe, PeeWee Reese, Duke Snyder and how the Dodgers moved from Brooklyn to Los Angeles. Apparently, that was a big deal.

    The seminal event that sealed me a Dodger fan occurred in October nineteen sixty-three. I was a fifth grader at Victor Elementary. That day the teacher pointed out that it was the first day of the World Series. "How many of you want the Dodgers to win?" she asked. I proudly raised my arm and looked around to see how many others had their arms up. Not one. Apparently it wasn't cool to be a Dodger fan in Victor, something I didn't realize until that day. I felt very alone amongst all those Yankee lovers. I fended off mean comments and nasty glares the rest of the morning. My classmates assured me the Dodgers didn't have a snowball's chance in Hell of winning and at that point, I believed them. After all, the Yankees always won. During recess, I felt persecuted and found there were no other Dodger fans in the whole school. I know because I searched for them. Didn't find one. Not even a teacher.

I went home for lunch which I often did because we lived not far from the school. I was happy to do that because I knew I would be comforted by the only other Dodger fan in Teton Valley, my Mom. That was when they played the games during the day and it was on TV. To my delight the Dodgers were winning and the big Yankee hitters Mickey Mantle, Roger Maris, Yogi Berra, Elston Howard and Tom Tresh, could not figure out the Dodger pitcher, a left-handed Jewish kid named Sandy Koufax who was like a wizard amongst muggles that day. I remember jumping up and down with Mom and clapping as Koufax struck out Yankee after Yankee.

I stayed at home until the game was over then floated back to school. I was late, but when I entered the classroom I announced the Dodgers won 5-2, Koufax struck out fifteen and the Yankees were doomed because Drysdale was pitching tomorrow. I then did a very in-your-face version of the funky chicken dance. The Dodgers went on to sweep the Yanks in four and I would forever be a Dodger fan.

Because of Mom, Kenny and I loved to play baseball. We liked to play basketball too and we were pretty good players. We were very aware of Dad's younger brother, Blaine, and his athletic abilities. He was five years older than me and seven older than Ken. He played high school ball at Firth and was outstanding in football, basketball and baseball so he set the bar for us. He set it kind of high. We were no where close to being tall enough to reach it. Blaine went on to play college basketball at Ricks College. Unfortunately for me and Ken, God played a trick on us. We were the shortest Jones males in five generations. At five foot, six inches we were usually the shortest players on the floor which really aggravated us. We talked about it often, what we would do when we got our full height. Little did we know that we already had our full height. As pre-teens we fully expected to grow to be as tall as our father, who was six foot, two inches. All of his brothers were that tall, or taller. I really could have used an extra six inches in high school, but it was not to be. I read somewhere that people born with club feet usually are four to five inches shorter than they otherwise would be. Anyway, I always sort of felt that I was robbed. We blamed Mom, because she was only five foot, two inches.

To compensate, Mom taught us to play baseball which does not require as much height.

During the summers we spent much of our time playing catch or hitting fly balls to each other in the pasture. Ken was a fan of the San Francisco Giants. Don't ask me how that happened. I think it was because I was a Dodger fan and Ken just liked to pull my chains because the Giants and Dodgers were rivals. Like all good Dodger fans, I hated the Giants. Anyway, he liked Willie Mays and Willie McCovey, the Giants' big home run hitters. I liked Sandy Koufax the Dodgers star pitcher. So I would be Sandy and he would be Willie and we spent hours playing baseball.

It might seem odd to some that a little blond, white boy like Kenny would idolize Willie Mays and that his older brother, a right handed Mormon, would try to emulate a Jewish lefty like Koufax, but it worked for us. Sometimes we recruited Cathy, Tom, Nile, Ann, Bo, Wayne and Jimmy to stand near the bases and act like they knew what was going on. Other times our cousins Ava and Betty would join us and we would play a real game. Mom would join in too and then it got really fun.

Unfortunately for us, organized baseball was largely disorganized in Victor. Not surprising, since it seems like we had snow on the ground nine months of every year. It got better a few years later for Tom and Nile when Leland Bressler became coach. But for Ken and me we were mainly coachless, and if we could get a ride to Driggs we managed to play a grand total of five or six games per summer. Our coaches tended to be the older members of the team.

It was during the disorganized baseball days that a truly memorable event occurred—Kenny's unassisted triple play.

We were playing the Pratt Ward at their field in

Alta, Wyoming. The teams were organized according to LDS Church wards then. The interesting thing about Pratt is that they never won a game. Miracles occurred at the oddest points in a ball game to keep them winless because, as we all knew, God didn't like them. They always lost and the events of that particular day went a long way to reinforcing that perception. I usually don't believe in divine intervention in baseball games unless the Pratt Ward is involved. Whenever we played Pratt we could always count on putting one in the win column. They were cursed. Nevertheless, it was a close game. I was pitching for Victor; Kenny was playing third. The game had turned into a real pitcher's duel. We were leading 17-16 in the bottom of the fifth inning, the last inning. We only played five.

    I was tired. Over the course of five innings it takes a lot of pitches to walk in 16 runs. Anyway, in the bottom of the fifth we finally got to the point where the score was 17-16, the bases were loaded and there were no outs. Kenny was playing third base and finally had enough. He walked over to the pitcher's mound to give me a pep talk.

    "Big brother, we are in serious trouble" he said. "You are killing us. In case you haven't noticed we have the bases loaded and no outs. If you walk in one more run the game will be tied. If you walk in two more, Pratt wins and we will be the laughingstock of all of baseball. Nobody loses to Pratt. It's not possible."

He paused for effect and grabbed the ball out of my glove and shook it in my face. "Throw the damn ball over the plate. No more curves. No more screwballs. No more spitters. No more acting like you're trying to be Sandy damn Koufax. Throw a strike. If they hit it, maybe a miracle will happen and we'll win this game."

He shoved the ball back into my glove and stalked back to third base.

The Pratt hitter was waiting. He was a big, strong farm kid and he looked well fed, but hungry and he could smell the first win in Pratt Ward history coming. I took a deep breath, wound up and threw the ball. It was the best pitch I'd made all day. Unfortunately, it went right down the middle of the plate.

The Pratt kid already had struck out three times. But this time his swing was as smooth and sweet as (should I say it?), yes, Willie Mays'. He murdered that pitch. The ball came off the fat part of his bat like a bullet, a line drive about three feet off the ground down the third base line straight at Kenny's head. It was pure justice. Kenny got just what he wanted and I had a perfect view of the entire miracle from my spot on the pitcher's mound. Kenny's reaction was total and complete reflex. Rather than try to catch it he simply threw up his left arm and twisted his body to the right to protect his head. Had that ball hit him in the head, it would have killed him. Instead, the ball buried itself in his left armpit causing his arm to snap downward and trap the ball (one out). With his right hand, Kenny's plucked the ball from his left armpit as he stumbled onto third base where the runner had broken toward home plate and was too slow getting back (two outs). I'm not sure who was more surprised; Kenny or the runner from second base as Kenny ran him down between third and second and tagged him on the butt for the third out. Moses parting the Red Sea couldn't have been more spectacular.

That night as we were drifting off to sleep Kenny admitted that his armpit hurt.

"I've got a great big bruise," he said.

"That ball hit you pretty hard," I said. "I was surprised you held onto it."

"It was a total accident you know. I didn't mean to catch it with my armpit."

"You could have fooled me," I said. "It looked to me like you've been practicing catching balls with your armpit. You might have started a new baseball trend. No more gloves. Us Victor boys will just use our armpits to snag those ground balls and line drives from now on."

"Oh shut up you surly son of a bitch."

"Go to sleep you mean little bastard."

(Left) Eva Jemmett and Elmer Jones.

(Lower left) Fernie Annette Moore.

(Below) Peter Herman Lott.

(Right) Fern Lott and Jerry Jones.

(Below) Brothers, sisters and parents in August 1973: (Front row left to right): Cathy, Mom (Fern), Dad (Jerry), Annie.

(Back row): Russell, Tom, Kenny, Nile.

(Top) Kenny (circa 1962).

(Middle) The Posse: Gary Matkin (1954-1969), Kenny, and cousin Bo Weekes (1954-1973) on Pole Ridge during August, 1968, on our way to Upper Palisades Lake. We all thought we were bulletproof. All three died within seven years.

(Left) Kenny and Russ (circa 1959).

Kenny's first grade photo.

Brent Jones (1947-1968).

(Above) Grandma, Dad, uncles and aunts circa 1988.
(Front row left to right): Gordon, Fay, Grandma (Eva Jemmett Jones) Connie, Jerry (Dad). Middle row: Jewell, Ted, Mel, Randy, Blaine. Back row: Boyd.
Not pictured: Joyce (1925-1939), Brent (1947-1968), Grandpa (Elmer Jones 1895-1953).

SHE WAS A KILLER

We had pets, mainly cats and horses. We had dogs too, but, with one exception, they came and went fairly quickly and didn't have much staying power. The main thing I remember about our dogs was that they would scare up a skunk in the middle of the night and chase it under the house where they would harass it until it sprayed. There was a hole in the house's foundation almost directly under the boys' bedroom. When the skunk sprayed it was intense and the smell sometimes lingered for days. We swore like sailors when that happened.

My Dad had a love/hate relationship with dogs. He liked them and had no objection to us having a dog, but if the dogs stepped out of line and say, chased one of Dad's horses, its life expectancy dropped dramatically. The reason for that is that we had barbed wire fences around our pasture and dogs could easily chase the horses into the fence where they would get cut badly. Since the horses were far more valuable than a dog, if they chased the horses and Dad saw it they likely would eat a bullet.

I remember as a boy having a number of dogs—Old Shep, Old Bob, Old Nick . . . Old Bullet. They all met similar fates. Each became a problem in some way, or got sick. The nearest veterinarian was seventy-five miles away so the solution was to put them out of their misery as quickly as possible.

There was one dog, however, that whenever the time of reckoning came, refused to die. He had a tenacity for life unmatched by any dog I've ever known. Dad couldn't even kill him. My next-door-neighbor cousins got him as a pup and named him Snow because he was white. They didn't know Old Snow would become a legend.

Old Snow lived in the gray area between good dog and bad dog. He always was in trouble. If he wasn't chasing cars, he was harassing livestock or biting kids. One year Old Snow got run over by a car he was chasing. Somehow my cousins nursed him back to health. A year later, Dad caught Snow chasing his horses and shot him with a .22 rifle. No vital organs were hit, but Old Snow bled a lot. Before Dad could finish him off Snow crawled under a shed. A few days later he crawled out from under the shed and somebody fed him. I think it was Dad.

The next winter some children were riding a snowmobile around a snow-covered field near our place. Old Snow chased them and pulled one little boy off the snowmobile ripping his coat and scaring him half to death. Dad saw it, got his gun out and shot Old Snow again. Old Snow bled a lot and crawled under the shed.

For Snow to survive two bullets fired by my Dad was

more than a small miracle because, as I've mentioned, Dad was an expert rifleman. Dad was more impressed by it than anyone so when Snow survived two shootings Dad pronounced him trained. Snow quit chasing livestock and kids and from then on concentrated on cars. Dad had no problem with that. If Snow tried to rip the tires off a Chevy, it wasn't any of Dad's business.

Despite Snow's superior survival skills, he didn't get any smarter with age. While chasing cars the next summer he actually caught one, which then ran over him and broke him up badly. Again, he refused to die and fought back, but from then on when he walked his hind legs were not in sync with his front and sometimes his back end outran his front end. But he still chased cars.

How can you not admire that sort of doggedness? I actually hoped he could take down the next Buick he went up against, but by then he was pretty much spent.

He should have been put down then, but no one could do it. He was simply too heroic of a car chaser to shoot. Besides, Dad was convinced a bullet wouldn't work. So my cousins kept feeding him and he finally died of old age. He was the equivalent of one hundred and six in man years.

I wish he was around today. There are some irritating hydrids, Subaru and European cars the oxymorons drive that I'd like to sic him on, just the sort of challenge that a mongrel like Old Snow would love.

Other than Snow and the horses, the one pet that lived the longest was a tarter shell cat that Annie named Patches. We got Patches from Uncle Blaine. He kept a tarter shell cat that had a litter and he gave us the one that looked most like its mother. As a kitten, Patches did cute stuff like chase string and small balls. But it wasn't long after we got Patches that she endeared herself to the entire family, especially us boys and Dad. The main reason for that is that she was a killer.

One night after dinner, a mouse made the fatal mistake of running across the kitchen floor. We had a lot of mice in those days and Dad was constantly setting out traps for them with varying degrees of success. He also shot at them with our BB guns which aggravated Mom tremendously. He would sit for what seemed like hours with the BB gun trained on a spot where he expected a mouse to appear. In this respect, mouse hunting probably wasn't much different than moose hunting. Mom walked through the kitchen one winter evening after dinner while he was doing this.

"Jerry, what the hell are you doing?"

"I'm going to shoot that little son of a bitch of a mouse that's hiding behind the stove."

"Not in the kitchen."

"Well, he's not outside."

"Don't you dare put a dent in that stove or there will be trouble."

"Yes dear."

No less than ten seconds later that mouse stuck its nose out and Dad blew its brains out. Ken, Tom, Nile and I were really impressed and Mom stood there looking at us with a what-kind-of-a-family-am-I-raising look on her face.

Back to the story about the mouse running across the kitchen floor. This particular mouse was pretty stupid if it thought it was going to get away with such brazen behavior. Tom and Nile corralled it behind the freezer in the far corner of the kitchen where Tom was trying to kill it with the broom.

Somebody yelled "bring Patches. Let's see what she'll do."

Annie came running with Patches in tow. She placed her on the floor where she could see the mouse. Patches was on that mouse like a dog on a skunk. She leapt behind the freezer. When the mouse saw her it tried to escape by going back across the kitchen floor. Patches caught it right in the middle of the floor and it was all over. Well, sort of. Patches didn't kill it right away. She played with that poor mouse for about an hour. She would let the mouse try to scurry away and then pounce on it again. We watched and laughed. It was better than any television program, even Wild Kingdom. Did I mention we only had one television channel? Finally, I think the mouse died of fright. Then Patches ate it, guts and all. She started at the head and slowly chewed it up. She ate the whole thing and we all watched enthralled until the tail disappeared down her throat.

After that, our mouse problem gradually disappeared. Other things disappeared too. Like birds. One spring morning Nile, while looking out the front window, spotted Patches in some deep grass stalking a robin.

"Hey look, Patches is playing with a bird," he said so we all could hear. Everyone raced to the window just in time to see Patches pounce on the robin.

"Oh my Hell," Cathy said as Patches demonstrated she obviously wasn't playing. Annie tried to save the bird. She ran outside to rescue it and started to berate and scold the cat. The robin was still alive so she pried it from Patches jaws and it flopped around on the lawn, but it wasn't going to fly again. Annie spanked Patches while the cat tried to get the bird back. Finally, Annie gave up and ran into the house crying and Patches finished off the robin while Ken, Tom, Nile and I urged her on. Annie was as mad at us as she was at Patches.

Despite Patches' tendency to kill things, Annie doted on Patches and after a time we all acknowledged that Patches was pretty much Annie's cat. The cat liked Annie, slept with her, played with her and even followed her around like a dog. We all liked Patches. She's the only cat I ever saw that would fetch, but she only did it for

Annie. She was our kind of cat. Mom liked her because she solved our mouse problem. Dad liked her because he didn't have to worry about her chasing the horses, although one time I saw Patches eyeing the horses in a hungry sort of way. She was just fierce enough that if she had been a little larger I think she actually would have tried to take one down.

We had several good horses. The first horse I remember was a big sorrel mare named Lady. She was the first horse to throw me; I think when I was about three or four. Dad was breaking her to ride and thought he'd taken the edge off her. He asked me if I wanted to ride her and, of course, I said yes. He sat me in the saddle, took Lady by the reins and began to lead her around the yard. She deposited me in a heap and Dad picked me up, brushed me off and said he would work on her some more.

I was the only one who could catch Lady without effort. She would let me walk up to her and put a rope around her neck. I think that's because I was so small at the time and never saddled her or made her work. Dad had to chase her all over the pasture to catch her.

The best hunting horse we ever had was a salt and pepper gray mare. She was another horse Dad broke as a colt and we kept her for years. We called her Pepper and she was Dad's favorite. My favorite horse of all time, however, was an easy-going, golden palomino gelding.

The reason I remember this horse with so much fondness is that he was deceptively and exceptionally fast.

Dad bought him from Vernal Parsons, one of his friends and a local farmer and rancher. Butterscotch's sire apparently had been a race horse, but his mother must have been a homely old work horse. Butterscotch inherited his looks from his mother.

About the time Dad purchased him, Mom made some butterscotch pudding. That was the first and last time Mom ever made butterscotch pudding because it wasn't such a great hit with the family. We hated it. But all of us noticed that the pudding was the same color as our new horse. So he was christened Butterscotch. Our family had a habit of naming our horses after food. Besides Pepper and Butterscotch, we later had one named Peanuts. We never named any after meat, though, so there weren't any horses named Moose or Elk.

The reason Dad bought Butterscotch was because in those days he liked to race cutters and chariots and Butterscotch, according to Dad, was fast. When Dad brought him home, I remember sort of rolling my eyes and thinking to myself, "Dad is really going to be embarrassed." As I mentioned before, Butterscotch didn't exactly look like Northern Dancer. He was simply ugly. He had a rangy long back, short legs, stubby neck and a head the size of a ten-gallon milk can. Besides being ugly, he probably was the hungriest horse we ever owned.

If you stepped into the pasture with a bucket of oats in your hand, he'd run you down for it. Most self-respecting horses will play hard to get when you have a bucket of oats in one hand and a rope in the other. Lady was the prime example. They know you're going to saddle them and ride them for hours. Butterscotch didn't care. He had no self-respect. He'd do anything for a mouthful of oats.

Butterscotch wasn't entirely ugly. He had a beautiful white mane and tail that I spent hours currying and combing. I grew into my teenage years when we had Butterscotch, about the same time I discovered I liked girls. My first girlfriend was pretty and had beautiful long, blond hair that she spent hours combing and brushing. I figured we had a lot in common.

One night as the two of us sat together under a bright, full moon I felt an overpowering urge to wax eloquent. Her hair was so beautiful in the moonlight. I was smitten. So I paid her my ultimate compliment:

"Your hair reminds me of my horse's tail."

As you might have guessed, she did not remain my girlfriend. She moved on to someone who was much more eloquent.

Surprisingly, Dad started winning races with Butterscotch in his cutter team, which surprised the whole family because he looked and acted more like a big dog than a running horse.

After Butterscotch was broken to ride, we could put four kids on him at once if we rode bareback. We probably could have gotten more on if there had been room for them to sit. He was so easy-going that we could do about anything we wanted with him. His main concern always was finding a mouthful of grass to eat.

One summer when I was about fourteen, I started bragging to a couple of older boys on the Fourth of July. I told them Butterscotch was the fastest horse in town and if they ever raced me that in two jumps I'd be so far ahead of them they wouldn't even be in my dust. Never mind that I had never ridden Butterscotch in a race. It was bragging time at the OK Corral.

These guys called me out. In Victor, most all the kids with horses would ride them in the parade on the Fourth of July and then ease on over to the rodeo grounds afterward. About the time I got to the rodeo grounds they surrounded me.

They were juniors and seniors in high school. They saw my horse and figured I was all mouth. While they pranced around on their high-spirited horses, Old Butterscotch hung his head, cocked his right hind leg and went to sleep.

I admit I was hesitant to race. I was intimidated by these older guys because their horses really looked like race horses. But then one of them insulted Butterscotch. He said: "Jones, why don't you get a horse." To a surly son of a bitch those were fighting words, so I told those suckers to start their engines. We rode our horses to the racetrack that was adjacent to the rodeo grounds. It was basically a pasture covered with grass. About once each summer an airplane would land there so it doubled as an airport. It was about a half mile long and we only planned to race a quarter mile.

There were six of us. The horses sensed what was about to happen. The other five horses started snorting and bolting while Butterscotch was pretty low-key about the whole thing. He was not high-strung. Low-key was his nature. For a minute I thought he had gone back to sleep. He wasn't. He was alert, but calm. No matter, I was nervous enough for both of us. When we lined up at the starting line, he stood rigid, perfectly still, like a bird dog pointing. He'd been running in a cutter team all winter so he had a lot more experience than me and he knew what to do. I let him take over.

About then somebody yelled "Go." There was a bunch of yelling, and the thunder of pounding hooves. I'll never forget that sensation of speed, because in two seconds I was going about mach two and it was no contest, just like I had predicted. Secretly I was amazed, but I didn't let on how surprised I was. Butterscotch beat the other horses so badly their riders didn't believe it. They thought it was a fluke that such an ugly palomino could outrun their horses so easily. They insisted on doing it again. The second time Butterscotch was warmed up and delivered a thrashing that would have made Sea Biscuit proud.

At the finish line spectators watched as Butterscotch and I pounded past and then set their watches while waiting for the second wave to finish. As we reined our horses in and brought them back together to discuss the results one guy pointed at Butterscotch and said: "That horse is so fast you can't see its legs move."

A note of caution to readers: If you ever get in a horse race with a surly son of a bitch, don't lose. After that I was insufferable. I christened Butterscotch the fastest horse in Victor, and whether he was or not, he never lost a race with me on board.

DEAD AND BLOODY CARCASSES

Early one summer morning we all were awakened by one of Cathy's signature "OH MY HELLS" coming from her and Annie's bedroom. All us boys came boiling out of our bedroom as Mom and Dad rushed to see what could cause Cathy to start swearing like a sailor that early in the morning.

When we all arrived in the girls' room we immediately saw the reason for the commotion. Annie, who was about five at the time, was sitting on the top bunk with her arms around Patches. Cathy was pointing at Annie's bed, the top bunk situated against the wall with an open window near Annie's feet. Patches slept with Annie so Annie left the window open at night during the summer so Patches could come and go as she pleased which she obviously had been doing because there neatly lined up on the bed spread were the carcasses of nine dead and bloody gophers.

While we stared at the carnage, Patches squirmed out of Annie's arms, walked to where the gophers lay and began licking herself as if to say "you guys call yourselves hunters."

Finally, Dad grinned and said: "Looks like Annie's got her breakfast. What are you guys going to eat?"

"We all started to assemble around the kitchen

table while Mom and Dad went to get ready for the day. Somebody got out some cereal and milk. Bowls were passed around and we began to eat. As we ate, Tom said to Annie: "You know that Patches now is going to die of a broken heart."

Annie looked alarmed and began to tear up. "Why?"

"Because she hunted all night bringing those gophers to you and you're eating corn flakes. That's why."

"I didn't think about that," Annie said. "I don't want her to die. What should I do?"

"She loves you. Right now she thinks you don't want or like her gophers. Her heart is breaking," Tom said. "You need to eat those gophers."

"I can't eat nine gophers. Will you guys help me?"

"No," Cathy said, still disgusted by her discovery. She shivered. "I might eat moose, but I don't eat gophers."

Tom nodded thoughtfully. "You have to do it. She brought them to you. She loves you and she caught them for you. You should get up from this table, go to your room, close the door and eat those gophers."

Ken was looking at Tom his eyes bright with admiration. I could see his brain working.

"Take a sharp knife with you," Ken said. "That way you won't have to bite the heads off, you can cut them off. She won't care if you don't eat the heads."

"You'll need a spoon to scoop out the guts," Nile

added, charitably. "You don't have to eat those either."

Annie pushed away from the table, her face white. She walked to the knife drawer and got a steak knife and a spoon and headed for her room. She was so small and gullible that I almost spoiled the fun by laughing.

Tom started singing: "Great green gobs of greasy grimy gopher guts, greasy grimy gopher guts. And me without a spoon."

Annie probably would have eaten all nine of those gophers to save her cat from dying of a broken heart. She loved Patches that much. And, Ken, Tom, Nile and I, no doubt, would have let her eat them and laughed about it all day. I would have cooked them for her had she asked. Cathy, on the other hand, would not let it happen. Annie still was fairly little and vulnerable to suggestions from her older brothers.

Mom walked into the kitchen about then.

"Where's Annie?" she asked.

"She's having breakfast in bed," Ken said.

"Mom," Cathy said. "These guys tricked Annie into thinking she needs to eat those gophers or her cat will die of a broken heart."

"You little shits," she said.

Mom took over the situation like a drill sergeant. She got to Annie's room and stopped her before she started sawing the head off the first gopher. Then she got the entire story from Annie who still was terrified that her cat was going to die of a broken heart. The rest of us were snickering around the kitchen table when Mom came back and she was not happy. We were in for a long day.

    She sternly pointed at Nile, Tom, Cathy and Ken.
"Come with me."
She pointed to me.
"Go outside and stand under Annie's window."
She made Cathy hold Patches just outside the bedroom door and took Tom, Ken and Nile into the bedroom with her and Annie where they were instructed to make eating noises while she placed the gophers in a paper bag. She handed the bag out the window to me.

    "Get rid of these."

I'm not sure if the show was for Annie or Patches, but it seemed to satisfy everyone but the gophers. I walked west past Stratton's place to the creek where I dumped the gophers into the Tonks Canal. Nearly made me late for my haying job.

    This was repeated several times that summer. Annie would wake up with anywhere from three to seven gophers on her bed spread until Mom made her keep her window shut at night.

SPECTACLE OF NATURE

One spring morning Mom herded all of us out the door into the backyard to watch a spectacle of nature. We had an old woodshed in the backyard that robins built their nests in. A family of robins had a nest inside under the roof and the babies had been growing up quickly the past few weeks. The all were nearly as large as their mom and she, apparently, was tired of feeding them.

First, she pushed them out of the nest, all six of them. They didn't go far. They lined up on a two-by-four Dad had nailed under the roof inside the shed that he could pound nails into and hang stuff--tools, twine, saw blades, pieces of leather and so on.

Those fat little robins sat on that two-by-four until their mom pushed them off, one by one. They didn't go easy and when they did they had to learn to fly fairly quickly which they did. They weren't too good at it at first, but they learned fast. They had to because my brothers and I wanted to catch them. We caught a couple too, but Mom made us turn them loose.

I was a little wary of Mom after that. Ken wanted to know when she was going to push me out of the nest.

"I get the bottom bunk," he said.

"Don't get too used to it," she told him. "You'll be

following Russ soon after."

Kenny and I got into plenty of fights growing up, not only with other kids we knew, but with each other. Being older I had the advantage in size, but that didn't seem to bother Kenny. Whenever we locked horns he always gave me all I wanted and we both usually ended up with bloody noses. Dad told us that we should never let anyone "buffalo" us. We tried our best not to be buffaloed which resulted in a lot of fights, but buffaloes are big and hairy and blow snot out their noses, so it's hard not to be intimidated by them sometimes.

Kenny and my circle of friends was generally the same. Growing up, we played with Bo, John Matkin and his cousin, Gary, Delvin Humble, Vern Woolstenhulme and Royal Kay. We fished and hunted, rode bikes and horses, smoked our first cigarettes, drank our first beers, and otherwise got into trouble together. During the summer there usually were a number of other kids to play with who came to Victor from Utah or some other exotic place.

One summer afternoon Kenny and I and three Utahans, who were summering in Victor with relatives, got into a water fight near our place. It started with water balloons and was really fun for me because I was winning. From there it escalated to buckets and cans of water that we threw at each other. Then, when I had gotten the upper hand and drenched them with a bucket, the other four ganged up on me and attacked with the garden hose. I suddenly was drenched and not feeling particularly neighborly toward the other four, including Kenny. So I escalated the conflict even further by punching one of the Utahans in the jaw laying him out quite nicely. The others didn't think that was appropriate for a water fight.

The water fight ended with a bunch of name calling and me threatening to kick their butts all the way to Pole Canyon. They left and went to one of their houses to hold a war council. Kenny went with them. Mom and Dad were at work that day and I was charged with watching my little brothers and sisters so I spent the rest of the afternoon bossing them. Along about sundown, I saw my four adversaries walking purposely down the road toward the house. The showdown was imminent.

I met them in the driveway in front of the house. They informed me they were going to kick my butt. I asked them if they thought they needed four to do it. They allowed that any one of them could probably do the job, but that since I started the fight I deserved to have my comeuppance delivered by all four.

I was worried. I figured I could handle any one of the four, but I knew it would be a massacre if all four of them jumped me at the same time. I mainly was worried about the blond, curly haired one on the left who was being very quiet. Kenny was studying me very intently. I knew that if he came at me he could keep me occupied while the others kicked and punched at their leisure. He was just pugnacious enough to do it. I think that's what they all were expecting to happen as well. I braced for some real pain. One of the others drew a line in the gravel and dared me to step over it. I was about to when Kenny stepped across the line to my side and turned to face the other three.

"Sorry, you guys," Kenny said with an edge in his voice. "He's my brother and I won't help you beat him and I won't stand aside and watch either."

We all stood there for a few seconds thunderstruck. I remember looking at Kenny and feeling a great admiration for him. I think my love and respect for him doubled in those few seconds. I slowly realized that everything had changed and I kind of liked the new odds. Three on two was much better than four on one especially when the two are mean sons of bitches and surly bastards. I was about to exploit the situation and make them scatter like quail, but Kenny let them escape with their dignity.

"I'm hungry," he said. "I'm going to eat supper." He headed for the house. "See you guys tomorrow."

Later that night when Mom and Dad were home and everyone had gone to bed I lay in my bunk thinking about what had happened.

"We should have kicked your butt," Kenny said, from

the top bunk.

"I know," I said. "Why didn't you? You could have."

"I realized out in the driveway there's no way I could help those guys beat my brother," he said. "Even if you are a surly son of a bitch."

"It's nice to have a mean little bastard for a brother," I said. "Thanks for watching my back."

The bedroom was quiet for several seconds, and then Nile and Tom started laughing.

"Are you two going to kiss now?" Nile said giggling. Tom started making smooching sounds. Kenny and I jumped out of our bunks and pounded on their arms until Mom and Dad broke it up.

THE GHOST MOOSE

The Twentieth Century arrived at the Jones house in Victor sometime in the nineteen sixties. I'm not sure exactly when. It was a process. At the dawn of the nineteen sixties, we had electricity although I remember the two-seater outhouse in the backyard and the galvanized tub in the kitchen for baths and the wood cook stove that all went away with the advent of indoor plumbing. We didn't get a telephone until I went away to college in nineteen seventy.

I'm sure my parents weren't the only ones in Victor to vote for John F. Kennedy in nineteen sixty. According to the election tally, there were a few others. My Dad considered himself a Democrat and while he wasn't old enough to vote for Roosevelt when he was president, he spoke highly of Roosevelt and Truman and voted for Adlai Stevenson in nineteen fifty-two and nineteen fifty-six, at least according to Mom.

I loved to listen to Mom and Dad discuss current events and can remember topics like the Russians launching men into outer space, Elvis Pressley, Arthur Godfrey, the Bay of Pigs, the Cuban Missile crisis and the threat of nuclear war.

About a month after the triumph of the Dodgers in the nineteen sixty-three World Series I walked home from school at lunch time in six inches of brand new snow. As I entered our living room I saw my mother sitting in front of the television set looking very troubled.

She looked up at me and said: "You're a witness to history today son. President Kennedy was shot a few minutes ago in Dallas."

I forgot about lunch and sat down beside Mom. A few minutes later I heard Walter Cronkite tell us that the president was dead. The feeling was the exact opposite of watching Sandy Koufax strike out fifteen Yankees only a few weeks earlier.

When I returned to school the bell had not rung. I sat on the bleachers in the gymnasium trying to soak in what had happened knowing that it was very important but not really old enough to fathom how or why. Many of my school mates were playing games in the gym and upon hearing the news the president had been killed, I heard one yell: "Hooray, Kennedy's dead. Hooray, Kennedy's dead."

As the sixties continued things went a lot like that. Halfway around the world, there was a storm brewing in a tiny country most of us knew little about, more people got assassinated, hippies and anti-war protests became fashionable, but in Victor we were sheltered because most of it we just saw on TV. New and strange people began to show up in Victor, the overflow from Jackson. Californians mainly. But there were some New Yorkers and Texans too. Most of them had money, were smarter than us and they were hip. The world seemed so far away. But Kenny and I didn't have time to talk much about that. We were preoccupied. We had discovered the ghost moose.

I thought I was the first one to see it, but apparently not. I had been riding through the heavy timber between Mike Harris and Pole canyons. It was hunting season. I had my 308 Winchester, a lunch in my saddle bags, my hunting license and my deer tag to make me legal. I was planning to make a day of it hoping to get a shot at a big buck or an elk. A tag wasn't going to do me a bit of good for what I saw come crashing out of the brush about forty yards away. It was a bull moose the size of a John Deere tractor and making twice as much noise. When I said it crashed out of the brush, that's an understatement. It exploded and for a minute it felt like the whole mountain shook.

The rack on that bull moose was the size of the sideboards on Dad's pickup truck. It was massive, not that horns mattered that much or at all. Our family never really cared about trophies. Dad always reminded us boys the same way his Daddy reminded him: "You can't eat the horns." But dang, something that big is so fun to chase and that's what I did. I have wondered since then where that moose came from. It was bigger than a normal moose. I have seen pictures of Alaska moose and often have wondered if maybe the Fish and Game department transplanted it from Alaska to freshen up the gene pool. They've been known to do such things. Anyway, it was huge.

I thought to myself: "If I get that thing, it will fill our freezer, Aunt Vernessa's freezer, Uncle Gordon's freezer and top off a few other freezers around town.

By the time I slid off Butterscotch with my rifle, the moose had disappeared, but I could still hear it crashing through the timber like a bulldozer. I started tracking it. There wasn't any snow that day but it had rained. I never was a very good tracker, but it wasn't hard. That moose might as well have been dragging a plow. Its hooves dug into the soft dirt fairly deep and it went right through three and four inch dry timber knocking it over or breaking it. I heard branches breaking ahead of me. I gave chase. All day long.

I should mention here that our family felt an obligation to keep the moose thinned out around Victor. Since Great Grandpa Joshua and his sons wiped out the grizzlies and wolves we felt it was our duty, or maybe our right, to eat as many moose as we could. Otherwise, they might have overrun the town.

That moose went up the east ridge of Pole Canyon, through the saddles and draws all the way to the head of the canyon and then it went "over the top." I need to pause here and explain something. "Over the top" was a term my Dad used quite a bit, but I'm not sure if anyone else did. When you stand in our front yard and look south you can see the Palisades mountain range and there is a skyline that goes all along the southern horizon. It's visible to everyone in Teton Valley on a clear day. From the valley floor you can't see much beyond that horizon. Fog Hill is visible as is Thompson Peak, but there are hundreds of square miles of mountains and forest beyond the skyline. If we ventured beyond that ridge or skyline we called it going "over the top." Later in my life I came to think of going "over the top" as passing from this life to the spirit world.

But on that day, I watched that moose literally go over the top, but it was too far away for a shot. It stopped then and looked back at me casually as if I was some school kid to be trifled with, which in retrospect, I was. I followed it over the top. It went down the backside and part way up Fog Hill, then turned left into East Palisades. I followed. Sometimes it went right down onto the main trail that goes back toward Wyoming. It just kept going east and I followed. About a mile before the state line, it took another left and dropped down onto the ridge between Mikesell and Mike Harris canyons. I followed because by then it was getting dark and at least it was heading in the right direction for me to go home. By the time it got dark we were back in about the same place I found it that morning. Butterscotch and I were tuckered by then, him more than me. I would have bet money that moose lay down in the same bed he had the night before, thinking to himself "that was a nice run today."

When I got home I took Kenny aside and told him about the moose. We made a plan. He would go up Pole Canyon and wait in one of the saddles along the east ridge. I would jump the moose up again the next morning and chase it right to him. And that's exactly what I did. The same thing happened; the moose followed the same path. Late in the morning I kept expecting to hear shooting, but nothing happened. Finally I topped a little peak and found Kenny sitting with his gun in his lap and Pepper tied to a tree a few yards away.

"Did you see it?"

"See what?"

"The moose."

"Big brother, I'm thinking you're hallucinating. I've been here two hours and all I have seen are three chipmunks and a blue jay."

I showed him the tracks, not twenty yards from where he was sitting.

"I didn't see a moose," he said. "No moose could have gotten by me. If a moose had walked where those tracks are I could have rocked it to death."

We could see Pole ridge from where we were standing and about that time the moose walked out of a clump of trees, stopped, and gave us a long moose stare. It was too far away to shoot at, but we did anyway because it was laughing at us.

We gave up for that day, shot a couple of deer and went home, but we chased that moose most of that hunting season. Finally, one night after dragging our butts into the house after a long day's hunt that resulted in no moose, we sat down at the dinner table. Dad had a twinkle in his eye.

"I saw you two today up behind San Diego," he said. San Diego was a corporate farming operation that Dad had worked for as a boy picking peas. The land was located on the flat between Pole Canyon and Mike Harris. San Diego sold out years before to the Rammell Brothers, but Dad always called it San Diego.

"You were chasing the ghost moose," he said.

Then he told us about the times he had chased the very same moose and described the same trail we had been chasing it over and the plans he, Uncle Mel and Uncle Gordon had used without success.

"That son of a bitch walked right in front of us a half dozen times over the years and we never saw it," he said. "I think that moose is at least 30 years old and moose just don't live that long. There's something very strange about that moose."

We asked Dad questions and talked about it for a while.

"I don't think we should hunt it any more," Dad said. "When that moose dies, it will be the end of something. I don't know what, but I don't want to be the one who shoots it. Besides, it would taste like a piece of saddle leather."

So we stopped hunting the ghost moose and kept our fridge full of elk and deer. We left the moose hunting mostly to Dad, who would bring one home on occasion, usually a tender, juicy young bull that tasted pretty dang good.

Dad took his job of managing Victor's moose population very seriously. One time when he'd knocked one down, one of the cousins was helping gut it out. The cousin wondered out loud about the propriety of shooting moose since there wasn't a moose season and they didn't have a tag.

Dad responded simply: "They do better when you keep 'em thinned out."

In the fall of nineteen sixty-seven, I heard that some out-of-state trophy hunter killed a monster moose near State Line Canyon in Wyoming. Few people saw it, but those who did said it was freakish how big it was. It was some kind of record and after having it taxidermied, the man sold the head and rack to a Jackson millionaire who now has it hanging in his lodge. I don't know what became of the hunter or what he did with the meat. I hope someone ate it.

About then things began to change in Teton Valley. A big ski hill was in the works up near Teton Canyon east of Driggs. The developers said Grand Targhee would attract more Californians, New Yorkers, Texans and trendsetters to the valley and bring commerce and prosperity to everyone. And, we all would be hip like them. We all were excited. We were finally going to have money.

THE MOST EERILY SAD THING

In January of nineteen sixty-eight, I celebrated my sixteenth birthday. About five p.m. I was headed out the door to play in a junior varsity basketball game. The only reason I remember it was that as I left the house I met my Grandma Jones and Uncle Brent as they were coming in the door. I paused to give them both a quick hug and then I was off to catch my bus and I never gave the encounter much thought until months later.

Brent was my Dad's younger brother. He and his twin brother Blaine were five years older than me. About ten years earlier Grandma and her sons who were still at home had moved from Victor to Firth to live. Firth was about seventy miles away between Shelley and Blackfoot, so we didn't see them that often, but it always was a treat and a lot of fun when we did.

At that time as I remember it, Dad's brothers and sisters were beginning to spread out. His oldest brother, Gordon, still lived across the street from us. Uncle Mel and his family lived in Driggs. Uncle Jewell and his family lived in Jackson. Aunt Fay and Aunt Connie also had married and had moved to Southern California. Uncle Ted lived in Idaho Falls and Boyd, Blaine, Brent and Randy lived in Firth with Grandma. Dad's oldest sister, Joyce, had died years earlier of diabetes when she was fourteen.

Dad's youngest brother Randy was only a year older than me and I loved to play with him when we were kids. Randy, Blaine, Brent, Boyd and Ted often came to hunt and fish with us and when they did it was like Christmas.

It was unusual for Grandma to make the trip to Victor in January because the roads were usually snow-covered and slick and like us, Randy had school every day. They were making the rounds, visiting as many of Brent's brothers and friends as they could catch at home. Several months earlier Brent had been drafted into the U.S. Army. He had completed basic training and now his unit was about to be deployed to a little tiny country clear around the world in Southeast Asia called Vietnam. We all knew there was a war going on there. I remember talking about it in school and finding Vietnam on a map of the world. It was a long way from Victor and didn't seem that significant.

Anyway, Grandma and Brent's visit didn't seem that significant either. A brief hello, hugs, and good-bye is all I remember.

A few months passed. It was May, school was out and we got another visit from Grandma. This time Boyd, Blaine, Randy and Ted brought Grandma to see us and Uncle Gordon's family. I loved these family get-togethers. There was laughing, games and the type of energy that happy people generate when they're together. We played catch and saddled the horse for rides while Grandma and the uncs visited with Dad and Uncle Gordon.

In the midst of all this fun, Blaine was called to the telephone at Uncle Gordon's. Our family didn't have a phone at the time so if we needed to use a telephone we went to Uncle Gordon's or if someone called for us, Betty or Ava or one of Uncle Gordon's family ran across the street and told us there was a call for us. It had to have been a real pain for Uncle Gordon's family, but they were real good about it. Blaine took the call and when he emerged from Uncle Gordon's house he was visibly shaken. The energy that had been present evaporated. Smiles were replaced by frowns. Dad and the uncles spoke in low tones and shook their heads.

Blaine, Boyd, Randy, Ted and Grandma got into their car and drove away leaving the rest of us in stunned silence. I didn't understand what had happened so I asked Mom since Dad didn't seem to be approachable at the moment.

"A U.S. Army officer is trying to get in touch with Grandma," Mom said. "He has an urgent message for her. Your uncles took her home so she could talk to him."

"What kind of a message," I said.

"I don't know," she said. "We'll have to wait, but it's probably not good news."

A few hours later, a call came to Uncle Gordon who passed a message to Dad. Brent was missing in action.

A few days later a telegram confirmed our worst fears. Corporal Brent Jones was no longer listed as "missing in action." The designation had been changed and confirmed. Brent was dead.

Brent had been assigned to an artillery unit in Vietnam. His role was foreign observer. He operated a radio and had to be familiar with map coordinates and how to use a compass. He was near a place called Quang Tri on May twenty first, nineteen sixty-eight, in a personnel bunker with three other men when a weapon discharged accidentally into a box of illumination grenades causing a massive explosion. Two of the men got out alive, but Uncle Brent and a Sergeant Lemke were killed.

It took more than a week for Brent's remains to be brought home. The funeral was surreal. Brent's coffin was covered with a beautiful new American flag. I remember Grandma weeping and the helpless sadness that enveloped my Dad and his brothers and sisters. The funeral was in Firth and then we drove to the cemetery in Victor where we buried Brent next to Grandpa Elmer and Aunt Joyce. A sophisticated military honor guard in snappy dress uniforms with white gloves took the flag from the coffin, folded it with military precision and formally presented it to Grandma. It was the spring of the Tet offensive in Vietnam and thousands of American soldiers came home in flag-draped coffins, so the honor guard got lots of practice and they looked really sharp and exact in their movements. They then fired a twenty-one gun salute with the same rigorous precision.

My Dad and his brothers and sisters always seemed so stoic and resilient, but losing a family member this way was hard on them. They never fell apart, and other than an obvious sadness, there was no public outpouring of emotion. This period of mourning for my Uncle Brent, however, was the first time I heard my father cry. It was in the privacy of our house the first night we got the news. He wept like a child for his brother. I have to say it troubled me. The sound was the most eerily sad thing I had heard or felt to that point in my life, and it will haunt me to the day I die.

THE OXYMORONS ARRIVE

I learned about oxymorons in school in those years. For those of you who don't know what an oxymoron is, it's a figure of speech that is contradictory, like "hot ice." At least that's the common usage of the word. For some reason the term oxymoron stuck with me. It's one of the few things I learned at Teton High School that did stick. It wasn't the school's fault; I just wasn't a very good student.

I also became aware in those days that I was backward. I think it's because I grew up in Victor. There's something in that clear mountain water, or air, that triggers backwardness. It causes the synapses to fire out of sequence or something. I tried very hard to be hip, but never made it. I grew my hair long, wore pegged pants for a while, then bell bottoms and loud shirts, drank beer, but it never worked for me so finally I gave up. It didn't work for many of my friends and family either. We finally came to the conclusion that as residents of Victor, aka Victorians, we were backward and there wasn't a whole lot any of us could do about it. We were backward Victorians, a redundancy, two words that mean the exact same thing, and which emphasized our backwardness.

I mention this here, because it was about then that I started noticing the clash between the "newcomers" to the valley and the "natives." The new folks, the hip and trendy ones, observed that the way we did things in Victor was kind of backward, or at best, sort of hickish. We didn't like being called hickish or backward. The new folks seemed to be saying to us: "Victor is a beautiful place, and a nice place to live, but let's change it." Back then, there were more of us backward Victorians than there were trendsetting Victorians so things didn't change very fast. Over time, I nicknamed the backward Victorians redundancies and the trendsetting Victorians oxymorons. I had way too much time to think back then. And, as time went by, more and more oxymorons moved to Victor while the redundancies tended to die off or move away. It didn't take a genius to figure out what was about to happen.

If you are an oxymoron, you may think that I have bastardized the term "oxymoron." Don't worry about it; it's okay because I am a surly son of a bitch and I am entitled.

MOM KNEW HOW TO COOK

Dad almost got into a fight with a local rancher as they were having coffee at Yakkabodee's one time. I don't know when this occurred, but Dad told me about it years after the argument. Dad and several other coffee drinkers were discussing which cuts of an elk were the tastiest when this know-it-all said something like: "You have to have a pretty nasty tasting beef to taste as bad as an elk."

To which Dad responded something like: "You are so full of [barnyard excrement] that it's coming out your ears." I put the term "barnyard excrement" in brackets because I'm pretty sure that my Dad never once in his life used the term "barnyard excrement." He was much more literal.

Anyway, Dad and this guy nearly came to blows, but didn't.

I have thought about this a lot since Dad told me that story. If Dad would have thought about it a little I think he might have cut this guy a little slack because the care and cooking of wild game is something of an art form which not all people understand. We did because it was our lifestyle. A rancher who ate beef ninety percent of the time, probably didn't.

Dad taught us boys a number of rules about caring

for wild meat. He was meticulous about it. First, cut off the scent bags immediately (particularly on bulls and bucks). That is the first step in the gutting process. Scent bags result from the rut. Bulls and bucks urinate down their hind legs and then rub them together to create a sort of love potion perfume. It might work for cows and does, but it's not so appetizing to humans. Second, be sure to remove the windpipe or esophagus while dressing the carcass. Third, prop open the rib cage with a clean branch and on big animals split the shoulders with a hatchet to ensure it cools or it could sour. This is very important especially during warm weather. We learned to do these things and we had good tasting meat.

Another factor Dad may not have thought about was Mom. She could cook an old shoe and make it taste good. Mom had her own rules about wild game, the first being that if you get any hair on the meat while skinning it you will receive a Scotch blessing. I learned this by experience.

I don't know how many of her contemporaries were experts in cooking wild meat, but Mom was. Aunt Vernessa could, as could Aunt Ada, Aunt Ellen, Aunt Pat, and, of course, Grandma Jones. As a youth, I never could distinguish between elk, moose, deer and beef. It all tasted the same to me and at the time I could not understand why anyone would object to eating wild meat. We had deer and elk burgers and steaks, moose stroganoff, mooseloaf, and my personal favorite, spaghetti and moose balls.

I think I ate mostly wild meat until I was nineteen and left on my mission. While on that mission in Arizona I was served some tasty beef steaks and when I returned home I informed Mom that I had developed a taste for beef.

This is a good place to explain a little game Mom and Dad played at dinner time. When we cut and wrapped our meat we put them in meal-sized packages and marked the package with an "E" for elk, "D" for deer, and "M" for moose. Mom and Dad also had a code they wrote on the package to indicate the date and location of where the animal was taken. When Mom got a package of meat from the freezer she knew what it was when she cooked it and Dad would try to guess if it was deer, elk or moose and where he had bagged it. Dad would take a bite and say something like: "Ah yes, this is that little buck I shot in Rainy Creek." About 75 percent of the time he was right.

Anyway, the Sunday afternoon after I returned from my mission, Mom cooked everyone a steak for dinner. While sitting at the dinner table, Mom asked me what kind of steak I was eating. I guessed elk. It was beef. She laughed and laughed at me. I wasn't good at the game.

Mom and Dad also had a garden every year to give us kids a place to pick rock and pull weeds. She grew peas and beans, which she canned. Since we couldn't grow them in Victor, she also bought a bushel or two of peaches, pears and tomatoes each year which she canned for the winter. Each fall Dad brought home bags of potatoes and onions.

About once a week Mom made a batch of bread. I liked to watch her. I particularly liked to watch the yeast rise and then observe while Mom kneaded the dough, put big gobs of dough into pans and baked it. I loved the smell of hot bread. Often, Mom would rip open a hot loaf and give each of us a chunk. I drenched mine in butter. Loved it. I must have watched Mom make bread a hundred times, but never attempted it on my own. Despite Mom's bread-making prowess, she never was satisfied with the outcome. She would always find some flaw in it and would criticize herself. She would compare her bread with Aunt Ada's bread and always found hers second best. She was very jealous of Aunt Ada's bread-making abilities.

When it came to pies, however, Mom ruled. It didn't matter what kind—apple, cherry, pumpkin, chocolate and so on. Any type of pie Mom made tasted near perfect. Our family could devour every pie Mom made within a day. She never made just one pie; she had to make at least half a dozen. They were that good. Most pie connoisseurs will tell you that the secret to good pie is the crust. Mom's crust was as light and flaky and fattening as anything you would ever want to eat. Her secret? Lard. Fact is Mom cooked mostly with lard. She'd buy bricks of it at the store.

Once, Dad and Tom were staring hungrily at a thirteen-inch chocolate pie Mom had baked and cooled in the fridge. She took a knife and cut it down the middle. She turned the pie and was about to cut it into quarters when Dad stopped her.

"I don't think you need to make any more cuts in this particular pie," he said. He and Tom each devoured one half.

Mom never cut her pies into pieces any smaller than a quarter. All of us boys and Dad usually would end up eating two quarters anyway. I think Mom liked it when we would inhale her pies like we did. It got to the point that if you couldn't eat at least a quarter of a pie, you could just damn well go without.

Mom made pies twice a year, on Thanksgiving and sometime between Christmas and New Year's Day. Whenever she made pies, I always felt special because when she made pies she always made one especially for me. One lemon pie and half dozen chocolate cream pies for Dad and my siblings. The lemon was mine because I didn't really like chocolate pie. Not lemon meringue. I didn't like meringue either. Just plain lemon with whipped cream on top. I ate the whole thing. One of my favorite memories of my youth is my Mom's lemon pies.

I almost was the death of my Mom on two occasions other than my birth, but she was lucky. She escaped both times with only a broken leg. The first occurred on a cold winter night when I think I was about three. Dad and Uncle Gordon were somewhere, probably working. We were invited to spend the evening with Aunt Ada and our girl cousins. I was very excited to get there. It was dark and Mom was carrying Kenny, who was a little over one year old. A cold snap had frozen the tire tracks in the driveway into deep icy ruts. Mom stepped into one of them, twisted her ankle, lost her balance and fell into a snow bank with Kenny on top of her. She couldn't move or get up so she told me to go get Aunt Ada. I scurried across the street, knocked and was let in by Aunt Ada, who asked where my Mom was.

"She's coming," I said. I took off my coat and started playing with my cousins.

Luckily, Aunt Ada was pretty smart and she knew almost immediately that something was wrong and went looking for Mom and rescued her from the snow bank but Mom had broken her leg in the fall and had to wear a cast for a while.

The second time occurred in the fall. It was toward evening at our house on a beautiful fall day. Mom was busy making dinner and I was restless. I slipped out the front door and around the back of the house without being discovered. From there I dashed across the street to Violet's and ducked under the fence. I remember running through the pasture behind Uncle Gordon's house with the intoxicating sense of freedom. I had escaped. No one knew where I was or what I was doing. I was invisible.

I went to Uncle Gordon's chicken coop. I had been there many times before with Ava and Betty to gather the eggs. But that night I was on a search and destroy mission because I was invisible and intoxicated with freedom. I robbed the nests and broke the eggs. From there I went to Aunt Ada's garden where I pulled several fresh onions which I then put into the milk cans that held milk of their freshly milked cows. I then returned home to find that my mother had noticed my absence. She first called for me and when I didn't answer she went looking for me, but she went the wrong direction. She started with Aunt Vernessa's place, which required her to go through two barbed wire fences. No big deal, she had done that hundreds of times before. She found I was not at Aunt Vernessa's which really made her worry. She ran back to our house, again having to go through the barbed wire fences. As she was doing this, she slipped and broke her knee on a big rock. When she returned home I was there.

"Where have you been?"

"At Uncle Gordon's," I said innocently.

Later that evening, Aunt Ada and Uncle Gordon

paid a visit. They were very pleasant and nice as they explained to Mom and Dad what had happened to their eggs and milk cans. I remember my Mom turning to look at me. She was not happy. The fact that she had a seriously injured knee didn't help. Then Dad looked at me. He was not happy. Then my gaze met those of Aunt Ada and Uncle Gordon. They were smiling and appeared to be very happy as they immediately excused themselves and went home leaving me to suffer the wrath of my Mom and Dad.

About a year later (I think it was the same summer I used a piece of garden hose on Linda and Trina to enforce my displeasure with their constant teasing), I was playing outside with a small pole about eight feet long. I was trying to balance it so it would stand straight up in the air with me at the bottom. I was having little success when Betty walked across the street to play. She watched me and asked what I was doing while I tried to make the pole stand up straight. She wanted to try and I was about ready to let her when I lost control of the pole and it fell right on top of her head. She ran home crying.

A minute or two later, Aunt Ada came outside and she was breathing fire. By then Mom had arrived wondering what had happened to Betty. I tried to explain to them both that it was an accident, but I think I had lost most of my credibility with Aunt Ada, who obviously thought I had done it on purpose.

"He's just a mean little shit," she said to my Mom. In retrospect I have to agree with her, but my Mom defended me like Moms do.

"He's not a mean little shit," she said. "He's just a little boy."

While my cousins and I resumed playing with each other the next day, Mom and Aunt Ada didn't speak for something like two years which is pretty hard to do when you live right across the street from one another.

In the summer of nineteen sixty-six, before I started my freshman year at Teton High School, Aunt Ada walked across the street to our house to visit with Mom. Aunt Ada had worked at the hospital in Driggs and for Dr. Kitchener Head for many years as a Licensed Practical Nurse. Actually, she was called on often to do things that only Registered Nurses were supposed to do, but since there weren't that many available she learned to do those things and was good at it. I already told you how she sewed Kenny's finger back on when the doctor was out of town. But, that year she decided it was time to go back to school and officially become a Registered Nurse. She had learned there was a Registered Nursing program at Ricks College in Rexburg where she could get a degree in three years. She wanted to know if Mom was interested in doing likewise.

The idea intrigued Mom and before we knew it they both were enrolled and began school that fall. I remember the alarm going off in the mornings at four or five o'clock. Sometimes they had classes that began at seven a.m. and it was at least an hour's drive to Rexburg from Victor and that was on dry roads. They studied together as they drove back and forth. Mom hit the books every night. And it paid off.

I remember walking in the front door one night with Kenny to find Mom and Cathy comparing report cards. They showed me theirs. They matched up pretty good. All A's. Then they wanted to see mine and Ken's. Didn't match up so well.

Both Mom and Aunt Ada were on the Dean's list every semester at Ricks and when they graduated in nineteen sixty-nine, they did so with honors. I think that was the summer they delivered a baby in our driveway. A young couple, having their first child, was trying to get from Jackson to the hospital in Driggs. The baby decided to pop his head out about the time they got to Victor. The couple knew Mom and Aunt Ada were registered nurses so they parked right in our driveway and that was as far as they got. It was a good move on their part. Two very capable nurses helped that young mom deliver her baby and calmed the dad, who in my opinion, was very near the freak out stage. Mom told me years later that her favorite part of being a nurse was helping deliver the babies and helping the new moms in those first hours after their babies were born.

"I really like that," she said. "And I think that's one of my best skills."

TESTING MY DAD

As I grew up I spent a lot of time with Dad in the mountains hunting and fishing. Most of the time, however, we were working. Our lives were inseparably entwined with the mountains and forest around Victor. I like to think that as I grew to know my Dad and Mom I grew to know my grandpas and grandmas. I didn't really know my grandparents and I feel a little cheated because I didn't. But, my parents became who they were because of their parents and grandparents all the way back to the beginning.

On this day that I remember so well, my father, my younger brothers Tommy and Nile, and I were cutting posts and poles for a buck fence we were building for a rancher near Victor. Ken had begun working for Uncle Ted at the tire shop in Idaho Falls. Dad had purchased a few hundred trees in the Murphy Canyon area from the U.S. Forest Service, but we had to cut the pole-sized trees down, saw them into lengths and haul them out of the forest.

This type of work was common to us. Dad had been cutting timber his entire life and as soon as my brothers and I grew old enough he had taken us along to help out. It was hard work. The terrain was steep and covered with undergrowth. And we had to carry the posts and poles about fifty yards from where they fell on the hill to where our truck was parked.

As Dad would say we "hit it hard." Dad had the ability to concentrate solely on the task at hand. When there was work in front of him, he did it. I noticed as I grew up that Dad had the ability to accomplish in a few hours what would take some men more than a day. Oftentimes in my life when I have had tasks that stymied me I have thought, and quite rightly, that if Dad was present the job would be finished. Dad attacked work and he expected a lot from those with whom he labored. I think he was happiest when he had sweat pouring off his brow.

As a youth I always had summer work because local farmers and ranchers and acquaintances liked to hire me because they knew my Dad. They'd say things like, "If you're half the man your dad is you're worth more than I can pay you," or "Your dad is one of the hardest working men I've ever seen."

Dad cut the trees down with his chain saw and then cut each one into various lengths. Each tree usually would make one or two poles and three or four posts depending on its height and circumference. When he got too far ahead of us he'd stop and help us catch up.

The pole-sized trees the Forest Service had marked for us were situated on a steep side hill. Occasionally the Forest Service had marked dead trees. My brothers and

I knew from experience that dead trees were dry and therefore light and easy to carry compared to the green trees. The green ones were anywhere from three to four times heavier than the dry ones so obviously, the dry ones were much easier to handle.

We had worked hard for several days and were nearing the end of our task. At the time I was 19 and about to embark on my mission. I was in the best physical shape of my entire life. In the mornings I remember easily running up and down the hills sometimes as I went back and forth to the pickup. I actually was able to keep up with my Dad that spring.

By quitting time things were much different. The sun was near the horizon. The shadows were deepening. I don't know how many truck loads we'd loaded that day, but I do remember my 19-year-old body was dragging. I didn't have much left and neither did Dad.

Tommy and Nile were exhausted and Dad told them to rest while he and I finished loading the truck.

We had two trees to load. They were about the same length but one was dry and one green. Dad had cut them into six foot posts while I held the measuring stick and because of the way they lay we started loading the tips and worked our way to the butt ends. As we went the posts became thicker and heavier. Dad took a green post and I took a dry. Then Dad took a dry and I took a green. That's how we worked. Our rules to make it fair and not overburden any of us. When we got to the last four posts Dad took a green one and it was my turn to take the dry, which I did. I noticed that the last two posts would be about ten inches in diameter and would be heavy, even the dry one would be awkward to carry. As I made my way to the truck I saw Dad load his green post and then he walked back past me to get one of the last two.

    At that moment, for some reason, a test for my Dad popped into my head. Sometimes he broke our rules, but if he did it usually was to take the pressure off one of us boys. It was his turn to take the lighter dry post, but I wondered if he would take that monster green post instead. He often did stuff like that. I had heard somewhere that your level of integrity is what you do when you think no one is watching you. Dad had no idea I was testing him. I didn't say "Dad, I'm watching you to see which of those posts you pick up and I will remember it for the rest of my life." We were working in silence because we were too exhausted to talk. If Dad loaded the dry one I would not have remembered that day. It was his turn to take the dry one. He also had tools to gather up so if he had left both for me I would have understood completely. I realized that this impromptu test I had devised also wasn't fair and I felt guilty that the thought even occurred to me at that moment in that situation, but it did and I couldn't erase it.

    When I reached the truck I threw my dry post onto

the load and then it was time for me to turn around and see what choice my Dad had made. Was he the guy who would take the lighter dry post? Or was he the man who would take that heavy green sucker? I hesitated to turn around and look, but I did. After all, it was just a meaningless test that had just popped into my mind. So I turned and saw who my Dad was.

The surly bastard had both of them.

THE GREAT VICTOR DOG MASSACRE

Aside from the horses I think Dad liked Patches better than any pet we ever had which is not to say that he wouldn't cuss and kick her butt out of the way whenever she got underfoot. Dad liked to tease Patches, which Patches didn't appreciate, and Patches liked to climb onto the furniture, which Dad didn't appreciate and although Patches was very discreet about climbing onto the kitchen table there were a few times that she got caught. When she did Dad would swat her and send her flying halfway across the kitchen. She then would sit on her haunches and stare at Dad with that cat stare that seemed to say "if I was twenty pounds heavier I would rip your throat out." Dad would stare back at her and say something like "go ahead, try it, make my day."

Patches was house trained. If she needed to go she'd stand by the door until someone let her out. But when Dad teased her, she wasn't above using scatological and psychological warfare. Dad might have owned the heavy artillery, but she would fight back by pooping on his sheets or his pillow and then innocently climbing onto Annie's lap for protection. She seemed to sense that Dad would never rip her out of Annie's arms and blow a hole through her. When Dad would climb between the sheets at bedtime and find a present from Patches everyone in the house knew about it. Dad would cuss and stomp around the house looking for Patches. Patches usually would be in bed with Annie at that point. Annie would open her window and let her out until Dad cooled off. To me it was always one of those weird contradictions—Dad would kill any dog that chased his horses, but he would tolerate a cat crapping on his pillow. I never could figure that one out. She never pooped on anyone else's pillow.

After we'd had Patches for many years she got an infection in her right eye. It gradually worsened until it seemed to be life threatening. To my knowledge that was the one and only time our family ever took an animal to the veterinarian. Patches ended up losing the eye which the vet sewed shut.

Until then, dogs always gave her a wide berth because she was as surly as Dad and would shred any dog's nose that got too close. But after she lost her eye she became vulnerable on her blind side. One day while Dad and Mom were at work and the rest of family was gone, a pack of dogs caught her. Dad claimed they never would have killed her had she not been blind in one eye. He figured one of them came at her from her blind side and she just didn't see it until it was too late. The dogs drug her away from the house and left her in the middle of the road just beyond the corner where Dad found her when he came home from work. She was torn, chewed up and had bled out leaving a big red circle in the middle of the snow-covered road. It was obviously the work of a pack of dogs.

If the dogs had chased Dad's horses through a barbed wire fence and then ripped them to shreds and ate them, Dad would not have been angrier. This was the cat that cleaned out our mice and gophers and kept the robins from eating Mom's strawberries. This was the cat that slept with his youngest daughter. He teased her endlessly and she retaliated by crapping on his pillow. How dare those dogs kill her? Finding Patches in the middle of the road bled out was an insult that turned him into one pissed-off surly bastard. Thus began the great Victor dog massacre.

Back in those days, dogs were allowed to run loose in Victor. Most dogs were pretty well trained and would stay out of trouble. And, if they didn't stay out of trouble, they paid. Killing cats usually was okay for dogs, because that's what dogs do, but by killing Patches they crossed a line that only was visible to us Joneses. There was zero tolerance for dogs that chased cattle, sheep, chickens, horses, etc. They were shot on the spot, no questions asked. That type of unwritten rule worked for a long time until California discovered Victor. Then new people began moving in. The oxymorons liked the idea that their dogs could run free in town, but didn't necessarily understand the zero-tolerance rule for troublesome dogs and they would complain and howl when their dogs turned up dead.

They liked exotic dogs too. They weren't much for collies, hounds or working dogs; they liked pit bulls, rottweilers and wolf/dog hybrids. These dogs sometimes would run in packs and that's when they caused trouble and did dumb things, the dumbest of which was killing Patches.

After Patches was killed, any dog that ventured onto our place was fair game. Dad wasn't against luring them in either. Some men would have loaded their guns and started blazing away. Dad was far too wily for that. High-powered rifles are much too noisy right in town and would have stirred up the neighbors. Dad knew how to do it without causing a commotion; after all he was the son and grandson of the men who cleaned out the wolves and grizzlies in Teton Valley. He knew how to get a moose from the head of Game Creek into our freezer without anyone seeing him. A pack of domestic dogs was hardly an insurmountable difficulty. Dad didn't know which dogs killed Patches, but that was not a problem either. In retaliation, he simply killed all of them.

That winter the Victor dogs that ran loose gradually disappeared. It took most of the winter and not a soul suspected Dad. If they did, no one said anything. The dog owners simply found that their dogs didn't come home. And if you let your dog run loose you have to expect that at some point. By spring it was all over. The only ones who knew were family and the dogs that were dispatched. No one found any dead dogs. I found out how Dad did it quite by accident. I was attending college in Pocatello at the time and therefore wasn't living at home. That winter I paid a visit one weekend and while there walked back to Dad's woodshed to bring in some firewood. I noticed Dad had constructed a narrow path a few yards long that ended against the back outside garage wall. Blocks of firewood were stacked on either side of the path. If you followed the path for a few yards you would run right into the back garage wall where Dad had nailed a deer hide. The whole thing was hidden and, at first, I wondered what was going on. No one could see it but dogs could smell the deer hide. Below the deer hide on the ground partially covered with snow was a rusty old, steel-jawed wolf trap, probably one of Grandpa Elmer's old traps. It was set.

When I got back inside the house I saw a single-shot .22 rifle leaning in the corner on the porch near a box of shells in the window. It was far quieter than a hunting rifle so I knew its purpose.

That night while sitting at the kitchen table with Mom and Dad I slyly noted that it seemed awfully quiet outside. Victor is a very quiet place when compared to a larger city. Newcomers often comment that all you hear in Victor is the barking of dogs. That spring dogs didn't even bark because they all were dead. I observed it was sort of unusual to not hear dogs barking or howling around Victor.

"Very odd," I said.

"Not so odd," Mom said, glancing at Dad.

"People shouldn't let their dogs run loose," Dad said.

"Yeah, some surly bastard might trap and shoot them and then feed them to the coyotes," Mom said.

"Any idea how many disappeared?" I asked, somewhat brazenly.

"Eighteen dogs, three coyotes and two foxes," Mom said.

"Any wolves?" I asked.

"If you add up the hybrids, probably about four and a half," Mom said.

Dad shook his head. One of his unwritten rules was not to talk about missing dogs, elk or moose so we didn't discuss it further.

MY RELIGIOUS ENIGMA

We didn't go to church much. But while we were not religious we did have our beliefs.

Mom took Kenny and me to church when we were little, but I don't remember how often and it never got to the point that it was a habit. Dad never went to church.

In Utah, Mom and her family were active church members when Mom was growing up. Mom had a bandolo or bandoleer that she let us play with. As I remember, it was made of felt and we could drape it over our heads and wear it like a scarf. She probably got it as she went through the Mutual Improvement Association or Primary. It had little icons glued to it that signified various achievements. The ones I remember were the numbers one through thirteen that were arranged in a circle and signified that she had memorized the thirteen Articles of Faith.

When Mom was three months old, Grandma Lott died of a condition known at the time as dropsy. Mom didn't remember her. The year was nineteen thirty-two and the country was in the middle of the Great Depression. It was the year the family moved from Joseph in southern Utah to a little farm in Fielding in northern Utah. Fielding is near Tremonton. Mom's older sisters looked after Mom and her older brothers worked on the farm with Grandpa.

One hot summer afternoon that year a powerful storm blew in from the West. Mom's family called it a freak tornado because tornadoes are rare in Utah. The winds were powerful and the storm clouds dark and threatening and visually dramatic. Since Mom still was only a tiny baby at the time she was napping on a bed near a large rock fireplace in the main room of the house. Her older sister Belva wanted to show Mom the storm so she picked Mom up and carried her to a doorway so she could see the clouds and chaos the winds were causing. About that time a huge gust of wind hit the house causing the rock fireplace to topple over onto the bed Mom had been lying on. If Aunt Belva had not picked her up when she did the rocks would have crushed Mom. This was a family miracle Mom's older sisters told her about many times as she grew up and that she passed on to me and my brothers and sisters.

Most of my early religious training I received from my Mom. She understood the basic doctrines of the church very well and as I grew up I remember having discussions about them with her. She taught me about God and how to pray. One of the things she taught me that I remember most clearly is that everyone has a life mission, something that only that individual can do. No one else can do it. With God's help, we have to figure out what the mission is and then do it.

Mom and I had many discussions about religion and, when I got older, we talked quite a lot about plural marriage or polygamy. Even though her great grandfather and great great grandfather were polygamists, she was not a big fan. I have observed over the years that, when the topic comes up, most women members of the church express feelings similar to those my mother expressed. And, I have observed that the men, when the topic comes up, like to clam up and not talk about it, so that's what I am going to do.

I never have questioned the existence of God. I think that's because of my Mom. I always have known deep down, even during those times when I was not being good, that there is a God. And He is watching. I sometimes have wished there was no God because I knew at the time my actions were offensive to Him. Other times I have been angry with God because He didn't answer my prayers the way I wanted them answered. But, innately, I've always known God exists. I find Him elusive and subtle, but He's there somewhere. He's very good at blending into the background.

I think church activity was a conflict between Mom and Dad in the early years of their marriage. Mom would have gone to church regularly if Dad had shown any interest at all. Mom eventually gave up going to church because she didn't want to aggravate Dad. It's not that Dad was against it, he just didn't want to be bothered. He never said bad things about the church, but he also never talked of God, that I remember. The only thing even remotely critical that Dad said was a response to me asking if he wanted to go to the Blue and Gold Banquet when I was a Cub Scout. His response was disquieting: "Those people don't want us around," he said. I always have wondered how he came by that attitude. Dad was baptized when he was twelve and ordained a deacon, but he got sidetracked somewhere along the way. I wish I knew the particulars. I never was brave enough to ask him, maybe because I was afraid to hear the answer.

We had ward teachers who tried to get in the door once a month. Sometimes they got in and sometimes they didn't. Frank McBride was our ward teacher for most of the years when I was still at home. In those days we called them ward teachers. Dad liked Frank and when he visited they had cordial conversations and Frank always gave us an inoffensive message. Later, Mom and Dad had other home teachers not as friendly as Frank.

When we became old enough to make our way to church on our own, Mom tried to get us there. Our friends often went so it mostly was a social thing. Mom made sure we were clean and tidy and had our best clothes on with a tie or that Cathy and Ann had dresses. She wouldn't let us go in jeans and tennis shoes. She insisted we wear our best clothes.

Sometime in the fifties Mom purchased a Bible

from a door-to-door Bible salesman. We didn't have a Bible until then. This was a really cool King James Bible that came from a Mormon publisher because it had a Bible dictionary that explained Mormon doctrine. It had a section of four-color pictures of art by people like Leonardo DaVinci and other famous artists. The New Testament had all of Jesus' words highlighted in red. On the front cover was a picture of Jesus as a young boy with a halo. I loved that Bible and after Mom and Dad's deaths I begged it from my siblings. I still have it.

As Kenny and I grew older we borrowed a Book of Mormon from Aunt Vernessa because we were studying it in Sunday School and the teacher said we should read it. We tried to read it. I don't know how far Kenny got, but I got stuck in Second Nephi. I didn't bust through Second Nephi until I took seminary in high school and then I got mired in Alma. Religion sometimes is a hard concept for mean sons of bitches and surly bastards.

As I grew into my teenage years I became aware that I was a project for my friends and ward leaders. They worked very hard to get me to church. On occasion they would try to get me to early morning stake priesthood meetings in Driggs on some Sundays where they would serve breakfast. I don't think I ever made it to one of those early morning pancake socials. I think they thought pancakes would convert me.

Though my Dad didn't go to church, it would be

wrong to say he wasn't aware of church doings. Until the early sixties, Lynn Kearsley was our ward bishop. He was the local postmaster and a very good man. Our family liked Bishop Kearsley. I don't think we ever had a bishop we didn't like. Then Bishop Kearsley became President Kearsley as he was called into the stake presidency. So our ward got a new bishop. That was a big deal. I remember all my friends speculating about who would be the new bishop. That happens in all Mormon wards, I think, all over the church. Everybody had an opinion. And none of them got it right.

I think it was my cousin Trina, who came to our house on the Sunday evening immediately after the new bishop was announced and sustained. She'd just gotten home from sacrament meeting. As usual, we didn't go.

"Betcha can't guess who the new bishop is," she said.

My Dad was sitting on the couch when she came in the door. Without hesitation he said: "Dale Marcum."

"How did you know?" she said.

Dad shrugged. "Dale lives his religion."

Dale Marcum was seventh grade teacher at Victor Elementary as well as the band teacher. He taught me how to play the baritone, ordained me to be a deacon when I was twelve and generally was just a very good friend. I saw him like my Dad did, a good, honest man, and one who genuinely lived his religion and honored God.

But other than my Dad, the man who had the greatest impact for good on my life was Jay Calderwood. Jay was a close friend to my Dad. The thing that made me trust Jay was that he was just like Dad and my uncles. He loved to hunt. He loved horses and the outdoors. And he worked like a slave. He was over six feet tall and wore western attire, even at church. Even his white shirts were a long-sleeve western design and, except at church, he almost always wore a cowboy hat and boots. He was bow-legged and spoke with a western drawl. His younger brothers Neil and Mickey were my age. Neil was a year older and Mickey a year younger.

Jay was different from the other adults at church. He would play with us. He had nicknames for all the kids my age. He called me "Racket" and Kenny "Wild Thang." Whenever he saw us he'd get this great big grin on his face like we were his best friends in the world and then he'd box our ears, mess up our hair and threaten to "stomp a mud hole in our guts" if we didn't shape up. We ate it up. Despite his rough housing with us, he spoke to us like we were his equal and by doing so he earned our trust and respect.

Another thing that set Jay apart was that he never used coffee, liquor or tobacco and he went to church every Sunday. I, for one, noticed. After several years, Dale Marcum was released as bishop and LaMar Thompson became our bishop. LaMar also was a fine man and family friend and he asked Jay Calderwood to be one of the counselors in his bishopric.

Jay, Del Matkin, Bob Blanchard and Dad were business partners for a few years in those days. When I was a teenager, they contracted jobs with the Forest Service to spray trees infested with pine beetles in the Island Park area, or to build trails. These were jobs that had to be done in May, June and July before the bugs flew. Bug camp was like a city of 50 or 60 people. We lived in tents in Island Park for a few months at the sites we contracted to spray. We used horses extensively to pack the insecticide to the trees that were infested. We had nearly as many horses as people in camp. Everyone had a role. Some were sprayers; some were packers and some took care of other logistics. Jay was in charge of the pack horses.

One morning I was helping Jay saddle his pack string, about 10 horses. I was 18 then and had just graduated from high school.

"Russ," he said in his happy, jocular way. "I need to tell you something. The other day the bishop asked me to make a list of all the young men in our ward who are perspective missionaries. So I did. I want you to know that I put your name right at the top."

"Jay, why would you do that?" I said. "I hardly ever get to church."

"Just think about it," he said. "Just think about it."

So I did. I thought about it a lot. I never seriously thought about it before. I knew most of the guys from Victor my age were going on missions, but that seemed like a goal far beyond me. The fact that Jay Calderwood would put my name on a list to be a missionary surprised and flattered me. I did think about it and I'd almost think that I could be a missionary and then I would remember that I was a surly son of a bitch and surly sons of bitches can't be missionaries, can they?

Turns out they can. With a heavy dose of repenting.

That fall I started school at Ricks College in Rexburg. You had to be interviewed and recommended by your bishop to go to Ricks. At least back then you did and I don't think that's changed. Somehow I cleared that hurdle, but I think Bishop Thompson was pretty lenient with me. At Ricks, I was required to take a Book of Mormon class and since I was in college and not seminary I decided I would do the reading. I finally made it through Alma and blew through Helaman, Third and Fourth Nephi and before I knew it I was done with Mormon, Ether and Moroni. There truly is something that happens to you when you read the Book of Mormon honestly. I am a voracious reader and when I get started on a topic that interests me, like church history, I don't stop until I run out of reading materials. Once you get through the Standard Works, there are plenty of church books out there. I haven't read all of them, but I have read a lot of them, particularly those related to church history. And while doing all this reading I discovered that I, Russell Jones, full-blooded mean son of a bitch and surly bastard, have a long string of Mormon DNA. That's what you call an enigma.

Despite this enigma, things moved really fast after that and culminated in me being called on a mission in the spring of 1971. My destination was Arizona. I continued to change on my mission. I won't recount all my mission travels and experiences here. They're in my journal, but I will say that I had a successful mission and that those two years were key in redirecting my life. I learned new things daily and met thousands of really nice people and a few grumpy ones. I came home from my mission a very different person than I had been a few years earlier.

When I got home I don't think my family really trusted me. I understood. How can you trust someone who goes to church all the time? It might sound strange to you, but I totally got it. I think Dad was most perplexed. I don't think he ever truly understood even though he and Mom supported me financially all the while I was on my mission. Mom faithfully wrote me a letter every single week and Dad would say a few things that Mom would write down for him. He even wrote a couple of letters in his own hand. Like the rest of the family, my Dad even went to church with me--once when I had my mission farewell and once when I had my mission homecoming. Excluding funerals and weddings, those are the only two times in my entire life I knew of that Dad went to church.

People in my family like to joke when they go to church that they expect the roof to cave in on top of them. I think that's somewhat of a church-wide cliché and may permeate throughout Christendom. The usually unspoken joke is that they think they are such horrible sinners that God and angels object to them being at church and are waiting to punish them just for showing up. My experience is that I've never known a Jones that even made a brick wiggle so there must be something wrong with that perception.

I worked with Dad that summer and when fall arrived I enrolled at Idaho State University in Pocatello where I eventually graduated with a degree in Journalism. Along the way I made many new friends, met and married a beautiful girl (Barbara Havlicak) who, I have to admit, is perhaps the most tenacious person in the world because we're still married. At the time of our marriage in 1975, I had big plans. In some of my daydreams I became a multi-millionaire, owned my own newspaper and eventually became governor of Idaho and once, when the stars aligned, I dreamed I was president of the United States.

I didn't totally botch it, because today, Barb and I have four beautiful daughters, four fine sons in law, and nine equally beautiful grandchildren and (I hope) more on the way. But I'm getting way ahead of myself, and that's because I want to skip the next chapter.

KENNY FELL IN LOVE

Kenny fell in love while I was serving my mission in Arizona.

When Kenny graduated from high school in nineteen seventy-two, he went to work in Idaho Falls for Uncle Ted at the tire shop. About this time Kenny started dating Lorena Nash, a young woman from Driggs. He really liked her, according to Mom's letters to me on my mission.

When I got home in June of nineteen seventy-three, I found that Kenny was smitten, head over heels in love. I couldn't blame him. Lorena was pretty, she was sweet, smart, kind, practical, and she was in love too.

That summer big things happened. Bo was killed in August. Even though our lives were diverging at that point, his death shook us. It shook Kenny more than me, I think, because he and Bo were so close growing up. Death was never something we dealt with well and it's always harder when it takes someone so young and vital.

It was at this time that Kenny applied for and got a job with Union Pacific Railroad on the line crew based in Victor. His foreman was Joe Jensen. The other member of the crew was John Matkin, who was close friends with both Kenny and I all the way through school. The Jensen family now lived next door to Mom and Dad renting

Uncle Gordon's house. Uncle Gordon and family had moved to California. The Union Pacific job turned out to be a really good job for Kenny because it had good pay, benefits and he could live right in Victor. Seemed like the perfect fit.

I was getting ready to shove off for college at Idaho State, but before I could go Kenny and Lorena organized a cookout up Moose Creek Canyon for the Jones and Nash families. As we were sitting around the campfire that night, the two of them announced that they were getting married.

This, of course, was met with varying degrees of enthusiasm. Everyone was very aware that Lorena still had another year of high school remaining before she would graduate. Both Kenny and Lorena assured everyone there was no pressing need for them to get married other than that they were in love. I am certain there were many parental-type questions asked and answered in private after the cookout. Apparently, all questions were answered satisfactorily, because a wedding date was set and they were married on September fifteenth, nineteen seven-three, at the Victor LDS Church.

They rented a house from Ralph Thompson, Lorena's grandpa, right on Victor's Main Street next door to Lorena's Uncle, LaMar Thompson, who was now their bishop. Kenny went to work every day for the railroad and Lorena went to school every day until she graduated. I'm sure, there were a lot of people who watched the calendar very closely, counting the months from the day they were married until their first child appeared.

I went to Pocatello and studied. I found some good friends and was first introduced to Barbara Havlicak in a Courtship and Marriage class at the LDS Institute on the ISU campus. This course did not provide any college credit, but it was a load of fun because we were required to date other class members. While Barb and I were aware of each other in this class, we didn't date and would not until almost a year later. Once we started dating, it didn't take me long to fall in love and I proposed to her on Christmas Eve in nineteen seventy-four.

Nineteen seventy-five turned out to be a big year. The previous August, Kenny and Lorena announced they were going to have a child. That child, as near as they could tell, would arrive somewhere around the end of February. No one was more excited about it than Mom. She was not shy about saying she wanted grandchildren.

Barb and I set our wedding date for March twentieth so we were extremely busy going to school and getting ready for our big day. Cathy and Tommy were set to graduate from high school that year. It was a very busy spring.

On February twenty-seventh, Lorena gave birth to a

healthy baby boy. They named him Kenneth James Jones. Three weeks later, on March twentieth, Barb and I were married in the Idaho Falls Temple. On May twenty-second, Cathy and Tom graduated form Teton High School. Things were just popping for our family.

That year fishing season began on May twenty-fourth. Almost every day on opening day for many years, except those when I was on my mission, we all went fishing together. Dad, Kenny, Tom, Nile, me and any of the uncles and cousins who wanted to go. That year, however, we all were scattered. The day after graduating Tom, Nile and Annie headed off to Nevada with Uncle Gordon's family where they were having a reunion of sorts with the California branch of the family at Rye Patch State Park. Dad was working. I was in Pocatello nursing a sore foot that spring.

Kenny had no one to go fishing with, so he got up that morning, dug some worms, threw his tackle box and fishing pole into his pickup truck and went fishing.

He never came back.

The basic facts of what happened seemed pretty obvious even though no one was there as a witness. The day was blustery and cold like many spring days in Teton Valley. Mom and Dad said there were times when the rain mixed with snow into a miserable slcet. It was gloomy and cold in Pocatello where I spent the afternoon watching a baseball game on TV with my foot propped up. The weather pattern had been cold and wet all spring and I remember news reports that farmers who had planted potatoes were worried their seed would rot in the ground because it was so wet.

The northern boundary of Teton County is formed by a creek that flows out of the Teton Range on the east. On some maps it's called the North Fork of the Teton River. Locals call it Bitch Creek. During the spring runoff Bitch Creek can swell to four or five times its normal flow, heaving itself well beyond its banks. That was not the case yet in the spring of nineteen seventy-five. The water still was low because the temperatures had not warmed sufficiently to melt the snow at the higher elevations. Kenny would have been able to wade it easily, but I am sure he didn't want to have anything to do with the water that day. Too damn cold.

Over the millennia Bitch Creek and the Teton River have carved a canyon down through the lava rock. Bitch Creek continues westerly where it joins the main stem of the Teton River that flows the length of the valley. Miles downstream of the convergence of the two streams, the U.S. Bureau of Reclamation in nineteen seventy-five was building the Teton Dam, an irrigation dam due to be finished within a year.

I'm sure Kenny saw the creek from the railroad bridge he crossed numerous times while on the job. No doubt he noticed some very enticing fishing holes in the creek and determined that on opening day he was going to try them.

Dad explained to me what he thought happened. He said as Kenny fished along the bank of the creek, a portion of the bank on which he was standing gave way under him dumping him into the creek. As he fell he must have hit his head on a rock or something very hard and was stunned or knocked unconscious.

Dad said: "If the water had been high we may never have found him, but as it was, he should have been able to get out of there."

Dad said Kenny managed to pull himself onto a small sandbar with his fishing pole in hand where he apparently lost consciousness. No doubt his clothes were soaked in the cold creek water and he still was partially lying in the water. As he lay there the coldness of the creek water and of the day stole the warmth from his body and he died of hypothermia in Bitch Creek on May twenty-fourth, nineteen seventy-five, at the age of twenty, leaving behind his young wife and three-month old son.

Kenny was due to return home at four p.m. that day so he could take Lorena and James to dinner at the Nash home that evening. When he was several hours late, Lorena became very worried and called Dad. Dad wasn't too worried at that point. He had lots of experience with people getting home late from fishing and hunting, he being the culprit most of the time. He got in his truck and drove north to Bitch Creek fully expecting to find Kenny and his pickup stuck in a mud hole. When he got there he was joined by Uncle Mel, Lorena's father, some of Lorena's brothers and the Teton County Sheriff Pat Johnson.

They first found Kenny's truck. It wasn't stuck. They then searched along the creek with no success. They searched for several hours in the dark before finding him.

How does something like that happen? I have gone over this ten thousand times in my mind and never made peace with it. Such a freakish thing. So unexpected. Kenny knew how to take care of himself. He had ridden over hundreds of miles of steep, rugged, mountain terrain chasing deer, elk and moose on skittish horses, carrying a loaded high-powered rifle sometimes in blizzards and sub-zero temperatures. And he had worked hundreds of hours with Dad falling trees for firewood or fence posts using chainsaws and then snaking them out of the forest with horses, all of it dangerous work. He knew what to do, how to be safe. For him to fall into a creek no bigger than a good-sized mud puddle and not be able to get out was something I could not accept. It seemed so improbable, even impossible. To that point I thought I was making good headway becoming friends with God. This terrible thing that happened was an act of God and I couldn't accept it. I became angry, angry with God. Looking back, I realize it took me many years to get over it. Even now I'm not sure I'm over it entirely.

As a missionary I learned to pray night and morning and many times in between, but particularly at night before I got into bed I would get on my knees and pray, and every night I asked God to bless and protect my family. It's a practice I continue to this day. At the time my hope was, farfetched as it might seem, that my family would get religious, start going to church and eventually go to the temple and we all would live happily ever after. I knew some powerful Mormon families and saw the joy they shared together as active members of the church. I wanted that. I heard people recount experiences where their families had done exactly that. I wanted my family to know what I experienced as a missionary and feel the joy my beliefs brought to me. After all, our family is genetically Mormon. It would be natural. Maybe it was too big a miracle to ask for, but I prayed for it. I still pray for it.

Like my other brothers and Dad I felt guilty that I wasn't with Kenny that day. Any one of us could have helped him out of the creek and then we would have laughed all the way home. And we would to this day be telling wild stories about the day Kenny fell into Bitch Creek. And we would embellish like we do all our stories.

But we weren't there. For some time I guess mostly I felt shock. I tried to be stoic about it, but I cried a lot. One thing I never was able to do is visit the site of Kenny's death. I had trouble even driving past on Highway thirty-two. As the weeks and months passed the shock wore off and anger set in. Once again, I became a surly son of a bitch. The problem was that I did not have a target for my anger.

    Who could I be angry with? Kenny? Myself? Who could I blame for Kenny's death? There had to be someone and I finally zeroed in on the culprit. After all, I had been praying for years for God to protect my family. And the scriptures say "And all things, whatsoever ye shall ask in prayer, believing, ye shall receive." I prayed. I asked. In my full-blown pride I knew that God did not deliver. God was missing in action that day. He could have done any of a thousand things to protect Kenny. He could have kept that bank from caving under Kenny. He could have prompted Ken to take a few steps one way or the other when the bank caved. He could have made that damn bank cave in the night before. He could have made Kenny's head land in pile of wet sand instead of on a piece of granite. He could have made it a beautiful clear day with nice warm sunshine. He could have flattened one of Kenny's tires that morning. Or made him have a dead battery. He's God. He could have done anything, but He didn't protect Kenny.

And then, as time wore on, I realized it was even worse than that. Things like Ken's death don't happen by chance. It's too freakish, too weird, too absolutely an act of God. I realized the truth is that God made it happen. He softened that bank so it would cave when Kenny stepped onto it. He placed the rock in just the right spot. He made the water icy and the day blustery. He took Kenny just like he planned. But why? Was he punishing Kenny? And our family? Was he taking revenge for all those moose we ate? For being mean sons of bitches and surly bastards?

I nearly drove myself mad trying to figure it out. Some might say I made it. I have asked God about it, but He's not talking, but then again maybe He is and I just can't hear Him. It's like that between me and Him. When He speaks, my prideful self usually is not in the mood to hear. When I'm ready to listen, He tests my patience. I've learned over the years that a person really shouldn't fight with God. It's a losing proposition. You don't need any fingers or toes to count the number of people who've won a fight with Him, but as a mean son of a bitch and surly bastard, I have to learn everything the hard way.

After years of berating God, I finally was able to consider an unwelcome thought. It was an unwelcome thought because I have spent so many years nurturing my bitterness and anger at God that it's hard for me to consider an idea that requires me to give up my anger. The thought is that God might actually have been watching out for Ken, exactly as I asked Him to do. Maybe He was protecting him. Perhaps the act of ending his life was a shield, an act of mercy performed at the perfect moment in time that men, especially brothers, cannot see because our mortality does not allow that type of vision. I got this idea because a home teacher taught me that when God takes one of his children back, He always does it at the single most merciful moment and that "single" moment is not clear to mortal men, only to God. I have no great spiritual gifts that enable me to understand these types of things easily so it took me some time, a long time, but I think I finally have come around to this point of view. I'm beginning to see beyond my anger and pain. That's a big step because I could not even consider it at one point.

 That brings us right back to faith. Faith and trust are essential; otherwise, we're without hope. If Kenny's life had gone on another day, week or month, perhaps some awful event, something unspeakable, unthinkable or unendurable would have occurred, a fate far worse than death. Maybe Kenny would have contracted a terrible disease and died a horrible, painful death after suffering for weeks, months or years. I have tried to imagine a circumstance that would make Kenny's sudden death seem like an act of mercy. What would be worse than

Kenny dying alone in a cold mountain stream? To imagine that, I have visited some very dark places in my mind. I don't like going there, but I have done it a little. When I do, I withdraw as quickly as I can. Better to let sleeping moose lie and muster up some faith.

So, as hard as it is for a surly son of a bitch to admit, I probably have given God a bum rap over the years for taking Kenny. He probably was looking out for our whole family and especially for Kenny. And, while it's hard to comprehend, and even harder to admit, it is my hope that His act of taking Kenny will turn out to be one we look back on in the eternities and see as a loving kiss, delivered at the perfect moment.

THE HARROP'S HILL HITCHHIKER

About ten years after Ken's death, I was driving home from work across the dry farms between Newdale and Tetonia. I was struggling with my life, trying to figure out if I liked God or not. I think I may have been leaning toward the or-not side of the equation. Coming down Harrop's Hill I crossed the Teton River bridge and saw a hitchhiker directly in my path, hands clasped together begging for a ride.

I don't normally stop for hitchhikers and I certainly don't recommend it, but hitchhikers don't normally go down on one knee with their hands clasped together. He was kneeling in the middle of my lane. In the opposite lane, a fully loaded logging truck was bearing down on us so I couldn't go around him. I either had to stop or run over the guy. This man seemed to be genuinely in need and very grateful that I would stop for him and I didn't mind giving him a ride even though the stop was forced on me. He wore dirty clothes and had a long, scraggly beard. He carried a khaki-green army surplus backpack.

He didn't just jump right into my car. He politely asked, after opening the door on the passenger side if he could have a ride. I nodded and he got in, thanking me profusely. He smelled badly. It was obvious he hadn't bathed in a long time.

Most hitchhikers I see in the Rockies appear to be tourists with backpacks. They're vacationing, and normally have their hiking boots and a sleeping bag, so I don't feel obliged to give them rides. This man didn't seem to be enjoying himself.

As we got under way he told me that it was a good thing I had stopped for him, because if I hadn't he would have gone to find a place to die. He told me he'd been walking for a long time, and then mumbled something about trains, cold weather and misery. I don't remember a lot of what he said because he didn't speak clearly. His words were very soft and muddled. As he spoke, I kept asking him to repeat himself.

After a brief conversation we rode in silence for several miles. As we neared Driggs, where I lived then, I told him I would have to let him off. He began to ask a question. He was embarrassed and I could see it was difficult for him to ask. His head was down and he was staring at the floor of the car.

He said slowly and softly: "I haven't eaten for a couple of days and I don't have any money. As one human being to another do you suppose you could spare some money for me to get something to eat?"

Maybe I'm a pushover and maybe not. I remember feeling compassion for him and I told him I had a little bit of change. I took him to Hillman's Grocery store and stopped. It was the new store that Guy and Kent built when they grew out of their old store across from the bank. I reached into my pocket and pulled out some money. It wasn't much, but it was all I had with me at the time.

Most bums, when you give them money act positively underwhelmed, as though it's their dues. This guy was different. He sat there for a moment with that little bit of money in his hand not moving. His head was still down and he asked very softly:

"Why would a person like you do this for someone like me?"

That question opened me up right down to the marrow. I didn't know what to say. I was totally stumped. He assumed I was someone respectable. He made me feel a lot more important than I really was. He obviously didn't know I was a surly son of a bitch. Finally, I shrugged and said the only thing I could think of: "You're a brother."

He nodded and got out of the car. Before he shut the door he leaned back down and said something about as profound, clear and eloquent as anything I have ever heard.

"That's right," he said. "And those who won't believe will never see."

He shut the door and walked away and that was the last I saw of him.

PAYING FOR MY MOOSE

Times change. The mean sons of bitches and surly bastards are gone from Victor now. Like most redundancies, we've either died off or moved. Those of us who are left seem to be coming down out of the mountains slowly. In Victor, we've been replaced by oxymorons.

It's just as well because none of us could stand living in Victor these days. The perfect example of why we can't stand Victor anymore is that Victorians, who already were backward, are now forced to be backward by the now world famous Victor backward parking ordinance that was dreamed up by a bunch of oxymorons. Consequently, parking backward in Victor is no longer fun like it used to be; it's annoying—not only to current Victorians, but to former Victorians. We can be backward without anyone forcing us. I think the oxymorons were hoping that doubling down on the backward thing would make the old Victorians trendy. They must have been thinking that two backwards would make an oxymoron. As you and I know, two backwards make a redundancy, not an oxymoron. And now Victorians are less neighborly.

Today, I don't know of anywhere in Idaho, the Northwest or the entire United States that boasts backward parking on Main Street, except for Victor. So does that make Victor trendy or hickish? You decide. One thing I know for certain: it's damned annoying. The conspiracy theorist in me thinks they did it to drive all of us poor redundancies away in favor of rich oxymorons.

During the summer the oxymorons play loud music on Thursday nights in the Victor city park. Hundreds of fashionable people from New York, London, Paris and Jackson come to listen to the music. It's a sight to behold and totally out of character for Victor. Hundreds of cars neatly parked backward like a scene out of the movie *Pleasantville.* And the visitors say chic things like: "Wow, Victor is a hip place. They play annoyingly loud music and park backward."

For me, this begets less fondness and sentimentality for Victor.

Most of the old Victorians don't know what to do about all this trendiness. They want to be law-abiding citizens, but this backward parking thing just goes against the grain in so many ways. Many have decided that resistance is futile and are assimilating into the new oxymoron collective where everyone parks backward like good little lemmings.

All, that is, except for my hero. I'm not sure who he is, but I like him. It may be the ghost of some backward Victorian who has come back from the grave to haunt the oxymorons for being so annoying. Maybe he's family.

That would be good, a ghostly mean son of a bitch and surly bastard come back to haunt the oxymorons.

The more I think about it, the more I'm sure he's a relative. He's familiar because he has embraced the old Victorian parking philosophy of "I'll park any damn way I feel like and to Hell with you if you don't like it." Sometimes, when I go to Victor I see his truck parked backward which would be frontward and normal in most towns. I never see him though, only his truck.

In nineteen eighty-four, nine years after Kenny's death, Mom died. She always said she never wanted to get old and become a burden to anyone, especially us kids. She got her wish on that one. She went as quickly as Kenny did. One Sunday afternoon, August nineteenth, she had a massive heart attack and collapsed. Dad rushed her to the hospital in Driggs, but it was too late. She was only fifty-two.

About a month after Mom died, Nile disappeared. He had been having troubles since returning from the service. The episodes of hearing voices and seeing things that the rest of us never saw or heard progressively got worse. He surfaced a few months later after spending some time in the VA Hospital in Montana. He returned to Victor and lived with Dad, but was prone to disappearing for weeks and months at a time and usually turning up at a VA Hospital somewhere. None of us knew what to do. He seemed distant and angry, a typical surly son of a bitch on steroids. He worried all of us, especially Dad. Finally, after more than ten years of being in and out of the hospital and a hundred different diagnoses, we learned that Nile had a brain tumor, a big, ugly, nasty one, a large mass with many tentacles going outward. It was inoperable and terminal.

For most people that would be incredibly bad news. For Nile, it seemed to me that he felt relief. He finally knew what his problem was and we had an explanation for his erratic behavior over the years. He spent the next year at the Good Samaritan Hospital in Idaho Falls. They kept him as comfortable as possible. He finally tried to communicate with us, but by then the tumor had invaded the speech center of his brain and he found it hard to find words to express himself. He died on September twenty-third, nineteen ninety-five. He was thirty-six and never had married.

Dad stuck around for a few more years, but he died on December twenty-fourth, two thousand three in the middle of a Teton Valley blizzard which closed the roads and made it difficult for people to get to his funeral. He was the first of our immediate family in Victor, and the last. As if on cue, the wolves and grizzlies returned to Victor, like they knew the day and hour that they would be safe, when the mean sons of bitches and surly bastards were gone. I suspect they eat a lot more moose than we ever did.

That means half of us are gone permanently. The rest of us only moved. My sisters still live in east Idaho. They're much like our Mother who hated the cold and the snow, but would never move. Tom has moved to Alaska, notably the only place on earth where it's still legal to kill wolves, grizzlies and moose. I still live in Idaho where I have become adept at evading the authorities.

Victor has become an oxymoron paradise. They come from all over, New York, London, Paris and California. Wolves and grizzlies infest the mountains, like vermin do, and have eaten enough of the deer, elk and moose as to make them exceedingly hard to find. Backward parking continues, as does annoyingly loud music on Thursday nights in the summer.

We sold the house in Victor so we don't get there very often any more. Since some of us are still alive, the grizzlies and wolves are not totally safe. But it's hard to enjoy Victor any more. The oxymorons take all the fun out of it. Now and then I get hungry for a moose steak so occasionally I pay a visit, and stock up.

It's not easy to run up and down those mountains these days. I spend more time in the truck than I should sipping on Diet Coke and glassing the open ridges. The moose mostly are safe from me though at times I get to feeling energetic so I might have one or two moose hunts left in me.

If I ever do go to Victor for a moose steak again, I probably will take my time. Before I take the moose I will feel obligated to pay for it by shooting a grizzly and smoking a pack of wolves. It's the type of thing that surly sons of bitches do. It's also a family tradition and skill. They do better when you keep 'em thinned out.

The End

Russell Jones is a fourth generation Idahoan and descendant of Mormon pioneers. He was raised in Teton Valley (the Idaho side) and earned a B.A. in Journalism at Idaho State University. He worked in media-related jobs most of his life as a reporter or editor for newspapers and magazines. He also worked many years in public relations. He and his wife Barbara live in Meridian, Idaho.

He is the author of *Traitors and Tyrants*, a novel about the Missouri and Illinois period of Mormon history.